AMAZE US,
O GOD!

AMAZE US, O GOD!

Experiencing the Miraculous

DR. MARK HANBY
AND ROGER ROTH, SR.

HOWARD BOOKS
A DIVISION OF SIMON & SCHUSTER, INC.

NEW YORK   NASHVILLE   LONDON   TORONTO   SYDNEY   NEW DELHI

Howard Books
A Division of Simon & Schuster, Inc.
1230 Avenue of the Americas
New York, NY 10020

First Howard Books hardcover edition September 2013

HOWARD and colophon are trademarks of Simon & Schuster, Inc.

For information about special discounts for bulk purchases,
please contact Simon & Schuster Special Sales at 1-866-506-1949
or business@simonandschuster.com.

The Simon & Schuster Speakers Bureau can bring authors to
your live event. For more information or to book an event,
contact the Simon & Schuster Speakers Bureau at 1-866-248-3049
or visit our website at www.simonspeakers.com.

Designed by Kyoko Watanabe

Manufactured in the United States of America

10 9 8 7 6 5 4 3 2 1

Library of Congress Cataloging-in-Publication Data
Hanby, Mark.
Amaze us, o God! / Dr. Mark Hanby and Roger Roth, Sr.
pages cm
1. Transcendence of God. 2. Marvelous, the. 3. Spirituality. I. Title.
BT124.5.H36 2013
231'.4—dc23   2013000386

ISBN 978-1-4516-6914-5
ISBN 978-1-4516-6915-2 (ebook)

My wife, Tess, has been an instrument of divine favor toward me and a true kindred spirit in this wonderful journey called life. God continually and thoroughly amazes me through her.

In regard to the recent books that Roger Roth and I have authored, Tess has tirelessly engaged in the many "behind the scenes" activities required to make such endeavors a success. She has acted as a personal assistant, manager, and cheerleader, providing the necessary computer and Internet acumen that are totally absent in my personal repertory of skills.

It is to Tess that we gratefully dedicate this book.

CONTENTS

CONTENTS

AMAZE US,
O GOD!

We Have an Amazing God!

God wants to expose your present world to a parallel world called the Kingdom of Heaven. He has created this Kingdom to bring forth perfect order, love, peace, understanding, and provision; and it is available now for all who learn to access its wonders.

The keys to the Kingdom of Heaven are meant for you and are available upon request. That request begins with the heart that cries, Amaze Us, O God!

—MARK HANBY

In our religious culture we have, for too long, made heaven and earth separate, isolated places. We live in one and hope one day to go to the other. This is generally true whether we attend a church, a synagogue, or another place of religious expression—or even if we have no formal religious association whatsoever. Since we disconnect our present life on earth from our hoped-for life in heaven, many have missed the influence and reality of heaven that occurs around us continually.

Rather than only desiring to someday leave earth and live in heaven, what if we were to aspire to bring the power, wonder, and provision of heaven into our earth? What would such a thing look like? How would it change our lives? Is such a thing even possible?

> What if we were to aspire to bring the power, wonder, and provision of heaven into our earth?

You've probably heard of "God moments," and most likely you've experienced many; these are similar to what some would call "aha moments." A God moment is when, in the ordinary activity of the day, some word or event triggers a spiritual connection with something that is happening in your everyday world. The following incident was one such "God moment," and it helped me understand the parallel world we call heaven.

Accessing the Parallel World of Heaven

I must confess that I am less than fond of middle seats on commercial airlines. Window seats are fine and aisle seats are okay, but delayed reservations had parked me in 26E, tightly ensconced between two rather large, very chatty folks who insisted on debating various issues ranging from politics to child rearing.

Dressed in my jeans and boots, I evidently did not meet their qualifications for conversational involvement, so for an hour and twenty minutes, I sat like a deaf and dumb referee at a world-class wrestling match, constantly readjusting my air vent to help redistribute their stale breath as it passed back and forth over my seat.

I was finally able to stand and stretch as the creeping line of fellow travelers retrieved their carry-ons from the overhead bins and slowly eased toward the terminal. Once inside I lengthened my stride—it felt good to walk.

The sign to Terminal D pointed toward a long escalator that eventually deposited me, along with a multitude of other obviously weary travelers, onto a platform facing several sets of glass doors. We waited there behind one of the doors for the train that would speed us to various parts of the airport.

Maybe I am, as some say, "way out there," or perhaps years of recognizing spiritual signs and anticipating spiritual manifestations arrests my attention at the most unexpected times through the most common occurrences. Rather than pushing forward to board the shuttle, I found myself engulfed in an *amazing moment.*

On one side of the platform, people were ascending and descending by use of the escalator from one level to another without effort. On the opposite side (my side), others were accessing a high-speed transport through simultaneously opening doors; the doors on the platform opening in perfect sequence with the doors on the shuttle.

These folks were being carried to a completely different area of Atlanta's massive Hartsfield Airport by taking only one small, but important, step. I was instantly aware that these magnificent manifestations of technological achievement simply mirrored the parallel dimensions of the earthly and heavenly worlds.

The spiritual or heavenly world is established, settled, and finished and is only one step away from our moving world of time and matter. Heaven and all its spectacular marvels already exist. We do not have to engage in some great effort to access or earn its bounty, we only have to find the portals—the places where the earthly and heavenly doors open at the same time.

> The spiritual or heavenly world is established, settled, and finished and is only one step away from our moving world of time and matter.

I was overwhelmed with the thought that in order to experience God's amazing, miraculous power, we only have to locate portals and enter when the doors to each of these parallel worlds open simultaneously. We then may be carried into our eternal destiny without struggle and without labor.

My ability to use the shuttle train, with its capacity to access all parts of that massive airport, required only my understanding and positioning so that when the train arrived I could walk through both doors and be whisked away to my desired destination.

If we are unable to locate spiritual portals along the

way, the climb and the journey of life are not only laborious but practically impossible. This book is intended to help you locate and access these spiritual portals.

Spiritual Portals Allow Us an Entrance into Divine Power and Provision

Try to envision what the world was like before man separated from God's divine nature. Picture an environment characterized by contentment, order, excellence, fulfillment, and eternal possibility. Now picture yourself being torn away from the divine source of this heavenly utopia to live in an earthly dimension where the struggles and harshness of life and your hunger for divine excellence cause you to search for access back to this hidden place of perfection.

We are each on a quest to discover the growing reality of God. For half a century, I have been teaching principles of divine connection. These are powerful principles for understanding the nature of heaven and earth, and they have helped many discover portals or access points into the heavenly dimension. These portals allow the perfection and power of heaven, in specific areas, to become manifested in your life on earth.

God quite simply wants to amaze us. He is so awesome, so powerful, and so great that anytime He shows us a glimpse of Himself, we are amazed. His love, His character, His provision, His wisdom, His graciousness are all attributes that He desires to share with us.

No One Has All the Answers, but God Desires to Share All Things with Us

Let me say at the outset that I don't know why God does everything He does. I, like many of you, have been engaged in a lifelong search to understand more of God and the miraculous. I don't want to limit that quest by the insecurity of always having to portray myself as being right or having to be perceived as having the definitive answer to every spiritual question.

> I, like many of you, have been engaged in a lifelong search to understand more of God and the miraculous.

I believe it is dangerous to try to have an answer for every situation and for every condition. Like an army that has advanced beyond its supply lines, our application of truth sometimes progresses beyond our understanding, making it difficult to advance spiritually. Faulty belief systems often originate from those who feel they need to have an answer for everything related to life and God. It may give them comfort to have God all figured out—to be able to put Him into a spiritual box whose perimeters are the limitations of their mind and faith—but this approach also boxes in God's ability to reveal His immeasurable love and power to them.

Although I certainly don't have all the answers, I do believe I have some keys that will unlock new areas of spiritual experience and help free you from the restrictions of misunderstanding. It is part of the human nature to search for answers, and as humans, most of us do that very well. What we do not do very well, in spiritual matters at least, is apply the answers we get so that they effectively change us and bring us to a higher spiritual awareness.

In this book Roger and I share many miraculous stories that are testimonies of God's awesome power and love. They have been selected to illustrate the particular subject matter of each chapter, but such accounts are by no means unique to us. When we become awakened to God's desire and love, we see that He is constantly doing amazing things—even when we fail to notice them.

Don't seek heavenly portals only for the excitement of seeing something miraculous. To do this is like standing on the platform waiting for the airport shuttle train but never entering when both doors open. When you sense or see the miraculous, always ask, "What does this mean?" and "What do You want me to do?" Questions such as these open up amazing portals.

The miraculous events described in each of the chapters of this book are, in part, the result of someone knowingly or unknowingly discovering a heavenly portal. This book is a tool to help you in your pursuit of the miraculous and its many facets. How you discover and enter these heavenly access points will vary with each individual and each situation. At the end of each chapter, you'll find insights to help you understand and apply keys for accessing spiritual portals, and you'll also find a section, titled "Personal Application," that will give you additional thoughts to help you internalize God's promises for you. I cannot provide a formula, but I can give you insights and understanding that will help you make connection to this divine source of power and provision.

Like a great house that has many exterior doors and windows, each leading to a different room or location within the house, so heaven can be accessed by various entrance points, which I call spiritual portals, leading to various areas of its amazing contents. I have detailed a number of these portals in this book.

Join me on this spiritual journey as together we ask Him to *amaze us, O God.*

CHAPTER ONE

Amazing Heritage

The life we start with comes from others but the life we live is molded by our own hands. God is a remarkable sculptor—He wants to help you.

Allow Him to remove your sharp edges and excess burdens by asking Him to "Amaze Us, O God!"

—MARK HANBY

Over thirty years ago, Alex Haley wrote the best seller *Roots*, tracing the ancestral struggle of his family from Africa to America. In so doing, he reintroduced an entire generation to the plight of slavery and perhaps as an unintended consequence, stirred many thousands from all races to search out their own genealogical histories. We each have a spiritual genealogy that is every bit as interesting and formative as our natural lineage.

Life itself is amazing and provides remarkable material for each one of us to tell our unique chapter of His-story. Those who came before us, for better or worse, have left us with the foundation upon which our lives are built. Regardless of whether or not we value or appreciate the particular groundwork that was laid for us by others, our life is the result of how we have built upon that foundation.

You've heard the expression "He was born with a silver spoon in his mouth," meaning someone was given many material advantages. Well, maybe you realize, as I do, that far more than material blessings, the greatest advantage any of us can have are ancestors, and parents in particular, who instill in us a thirst for God and the miraculous. But even if they did not, through our roots we can trace amazing events, whether we perceive them to be good or bad, that have the potential to unlock understanding in our lives.

We have a divine heritage given by God. We also have a heritage that comes from our ancestors. A heritage is literally the things that we inherit from our ancestors. This heritage is composed less of material things and more of the experiences, culture, values, and especially the faith that we inherit from those who have gone before us.

Intrigued by the Power and Inspiration of the Miraculous

I grew up in a family that believed in a God who was near. He was a God who was willing, and indeed even eager, to participate in our lives in a very present and active way. My parents had no problem believing in and receiving the miraculous.

I was just a young boy when I started hearing incredible stories and seeing irrefutable miraculous occurrences. These events caused me to ask questions and search for answers. I would ask myself questions like "Why do supernatural events occur at one place or time and not in another?" "Do these things just happen, or are they released by something we do or by some understanding we have?" "Are there keys to understanding and utilizing the amazing power of God that, if we understood them, would give us continual access between the natural and spiritual worlds?"

I was just a young boy when I started seeing irrefutable miraculous occurrences.

At a very young age I began learning about the amazing workings of the Spirit from stories my parents told me from firsthand accounts of miraculous testimonies and from my own personal witness. As a young boy I remember sitting in small clap-siding churches, in our farmhouse and neighborhood houses, and around smoky campfires and seeing God touch people in unbelievable ways. The following event is as clear to me now as it was the day I first witnessed it . . .

I watched my aunt Ruth closely as she scurried around my grandmother's kitchen helping finish preparations for Thanksgiving dinner. She was a phenomenal cook and was always chipper and happy. Her back was as straight as an arrow, and her gait strong and aggressive.

My mother and grandmother took turns shooing me into the other room. We had come for a visit, and my curiosity about the things I had heard compelled me to seek further evidence. There were lots of cousins to play with whom I hadn't seen in a while, but I was determined to see if Aunt Ruth limped when no one was watching.

The family story had been told over and over again about how Ruth, my daddy's sister, had been in a terrible buggy accident when she was fifteen years old. The horses became spooked by a thrashing machine and ran away, dragging her helpless body hundreds of yards under the overturned buggy as it scraped and bounced against the stony ground.

My grandfather Benjamin Hanby would often tearfully describe how his daughter's body was grossly twisted and her back terribly deformed. So serious was her accident that her right leg withered to the point that only the ball of her foot could reach the floor.

In a grotesque fashion, she would limp along as she did her daily chores. The incessant pain from that accident remained with her as she took care of my ailing grandmother and two younger brothers, one of whom would one day become my father.

On top of my aunt's accident, Grandma had been sent home from the hospital with six months to live after having two-thirds of her stomach removed because of chronic bleeding ulcers. With few material resources, the family was struggling and leaned heavily on their neighbors and the church community of the little Methodist church in Bruno, Ohio, where my grandfather was a steward.

This comfort was short-lived, however, because the family was asked to leave the church due to Ruth's "activities" during the worship services. In this case at least, the adage "trouble comes in threes" seems to have held true.

It was not that the church was being intentionally hurtful or inconsiderate; they just didn't understand what was happening—nor did my relatives, for that matter. My grandparents held no animosity over their removal, for they knew how fear and lack of understanding can cause people to do things they later regret.

It happened mostly when the congregation sang, and always when they sang "Rock of Ages, Cleft for Me." Ruth would fall out of her pew and begin babbling in a rather incoherent language. Everyone blamed the accident, and some diagnosed her as having epilepsy.

Often the amazing power of God tests our understanding and our will to adjust to the voice of God. Aunt Ruth, however, vowed that during those "spells" her body would become pain-free. No one really understood what was happening, but the entire family continued to pray for my grandmother and Ruth and to trust God.

It was during those lonely days that my grandfather's brother, Great-uncle Clint, rode up to the old farmhouse and announced that a makeshift shelter called a brush arbor had been set up in his front yard. A traveling minister had come to the area and was preaching that Jesus was still healing sick folks and filling them with His Spirit—"just like in the Bible." Then he added, "And I think we know what's wrong with Ruth!"

My desperate grandfather loaded the whole family, including my dying grandmother, into a wagon and drove the team of horses seventeen miles over the rutted dusty road to Uncle Clint's farm. There was a real excitement and anticipation from what they had been told.

They lifted Ruth out of the wagon, and when her feet touched the ground, her back instantly became straight and her right leg lengthened and became normal. She immediately

> When her feet touched the ground, her back instantly became straight and her right leg lengthened and became normal.

had one of her "spells," which witnesses claimed to be the baptism of the Holy Ghost!

My grandmother was also instantly healed and lived for another sixty-two years—she was ninety-nine when she died. These amazing miracles introduced our family to the wonderful world of the supernatural.

Now, forty-five years later, I kept sneaking into the kitchen with an eye on Aunt Ruth because I wanted to make sure it was real, and it was: she never limped or had pain from her accident since the day she was healed at that meeting on my great-uncle Clint's farm.

You Have to Be Willing to Look if You Want to See

And by the hands of the apostles were many signs and wonders wrought among the people.—Acts 5:12

God is a God of signs and wonders. In fact, many of the things He does fit under one of these two areas. Though many do not see because they no longer look, God is always speaking through an abundance of signs and wonders.

Signs are God's pointing device. Like a road sign pointing out the direction to a destination or providing information about the trip, so are God's signs. They give us information about how to connect to God and His manifold blessings.

God's wonders cause us to wonder. Some miraculous event occurs or some, as yet unclear, occurrence takes place, and we wonder what it means. Like the Virgin Mary when the angel pronounced, "Hail, thou that art highly favored, the Lord is with thee" (Luke 1:28), this miraculous occurrence caused Mary to wonder what all this meant.

God did great, notable miracles for my aunt and grandmother, but His purpose was not just to heal them but also to give direction to their lives and understanding to their purpose, and to set in motion an order of events that was to affect the entire family and the life of those, like myself, yet unborn.

Questions Often Provide
Keys to Portals

God not only did these things for my relatives but wants to do similar things for you as well. He is in the business of blessing you with the intent that you may know Him and gain understanding of who He is and how He acts. I asked myself, *Why did this happen at my uncle's house and not at my grandparents' farm? Why were they healed when they touched the ground? Why at that time and in that place?*

This miraculous incident got me wondering about how and why and in what manner the God of the universe interacts with His creation. Is it possible that there are spiritual keys that, if understood, would unlock the amazing power of God for each of us? I believe there are. But before we proceed to look at those, let's talk for a moment about the nature of signs and wonders.

> This miraculous incident got me wondering about how the God of the universe interacts with His creation.

Insights into Spiritual Portals: Signs and Wonders

Most of us, from time to time, look for signs. We want some external indication or confirmation of what we are to do, or that we are on track with some aspect of life. In and of itself there is nothing wrong with this as long as our ultimate goal is not the sign itself. If the sign becomes our ultimate goal, then we become lost in the sign and lose sight of what it was meant to confirm or what instruction it was to provide. We are not meant to live our life as sign-seekers. To do this is contrary to spirituality, and people who engage in sign-seeking open themselves up to the bondage of doubt and fear.

I once knew a married couple who would do nothing unless they saw a sign. If, for example, they thought they should take a trip to Kentucky, they would not go until the name of the state was given to them at least three times. It might be by hearing Kentucky on the radio or having someone mention the name to them in casual conversation. Their ability to hear the voice of God became lost in their reliance upon signs. Their entire life became dependent upon discovering some sign, and this fostered great fear and doubt in understanding or sensing God absent of signs, many of which were fabrications of their own mind. They of course are not alone in this. In fact many religions use external evidences of perceived blessing, financial success, number of members, notoriety, or social influence as signs that they are in the will of God. Sign-seekers will always find some sign, imagined or otherwise, that will support their desired results. But if we seek *God* above signs, we will have signs that bring confirmation and witness of God.

A Sign *from* God or a Sign *of* God?

Many, as in the example above, look for signs from God. "I want a sign to know if I should take a job," or "I want a sign to know if I should marry this person." There is nothing wrong in desiring confirmation from God about important decisions in our lives. We can think of most miraculous signs, however, not so much as signs *from* God as signs *of* God. By that I mean that they reveal some aspect of God that should make us wonder and desire Him as opposed to being merely excited about something we've experienced. God is always manifesting Himself in our world to those who are able to see that these manifestations are signs of His love, His nature, His intention, His wisdom, and so forth—in short, signs of God. They give us instruction as to who and what He is and attest to or confirm His presence in our lives.

Jesus in Matthew 16:4 said, "A wicked and adulterous generation seeketh after a sign." Literally, they seek one sign upon another. Yet God does provide many signs throughout Scripture, as in Mark 16:20, where it states, "And they went forth, and preached every where, the Lord working with them, and confirming the word with signs following."

God will confirm Himself and His word to each of us with signs.

In the story of my ancestors, the portal to their need was also a sign and a confirmation of God's word. My aunt and grandmother were not seeking a sign. They believed in God and had great physical needs. My Aunt Ruth's episodes in church and her and my grandmother's instant healing upon touching the ground on my uncle Clint's farm were signs of God's presence and confirmation of God's activity in their day.

Often things happen to us that we don't instantly understand. This is where *wonder* comes in. We need to see our lives in relation to God's purpose for us. Events that happen to us should spur us into contemplating God's love for us. My aunt and grandmother suffered some very difficult trials, but the end result was that God delivered them. This was not only a sign to them of His love and power but to the entire family and to myself, who was yet unborn at the time of these events. Having confidence in God through difficult circumstances will open for you a portal of deliverance as it did for them. They could have refused to get into the wagon. They could have said, "We've prayed enough, and we never get an answer." Yet regardless of their circumstances, they stayed true to what they knew of God. They were not seeking a sign and would have stayed true to their belief regardless of whether or not they were healed, but their belief and the timing of God's purpose did open an amazing portal for them, and it can for you as well.

> Having confidence in God through difficult circumstances will open for you a portal of deliverance.

Personal Application

If God's desire is to amaze you so that you may gain knowledge of Him and grow in relationship, then you and not He must make the adjustment to encourage these things to happen. A few simple thoughts provided at the end of each chapter can open you to the amazement of God.

At one time I remember thinking, *I'd like to return to that place in central Ohio where these and many other mighty things took place. Maybe there was something about that place.* Don't we all at times desire to relive especially happy or significant moments?

This thought was not unlike those of the woman at the well in the Gospel of John who had an encounter with Jesus that changed her life. She also was wondering about the place where God could be found. Jesus, in essence, said that it is not in a physical location but from a spiritual position that God can be accessed.

Think about a significant occurrence from the life of your parents or one of your ancestors. Recount it as fully as possible with as much detail as you can. Then ask yourself some questions:

Why did this happen to them?

How did they deal with the event and its aftermath?

In what ways did this event change them?

In what ways did this event eventually influence your life, even if you were not alive when it took place?

How was God in the event?

Then pray this simple four-word prayer: *Amaze me, O God.*

It is hard to know where you are going if you don't understand where you've come from. In your past you possess significant insights for your future. Amazing things happen when you ask to see the hand of God in everything, even the smallest things.

Amaze us, O God, by the power of heritage!

CHAPTER TWO

Amazing Wonders

We serve a wonderful God—He is full of wonder. His intervention through signs and wonders is not merely designed to do miraculous things for us but more important should stimulate us to seek to know this God who shows such great love toward us. His wonders should cause us to wonder about Him.

—MARK HANBY

I t had already been a very wet spring, the stock ponds were full, and streams were swollen to capacity. Now it was raining again and had been for the last three days. The news outlets estimated that an additional eleven inches had fallen in the last forty-eight hours. While this may not have been uncommon in some parts of the country, it was highly unusual for this part of Texas.

Our Sunday service was interrupted by water dripping in various places throughout the auditorium, and folks were moving around. I was surprised that any moisture could penetrate the four-inch tongue-and-groove spruce decking, covered with heavy commercial liners, making up the roofing structure.

After the service we learned that the roof of a new church building across town had collapsed, killing several people, and that the city engineers were on their way to inspect our building. They explained that the firm that had engineered the plans for the collapsed building had also designed ours, using an outdated moisture model that did not anticipate the extreme conditions we were now facing. With thousands of square feet of flat roof surrounded by a two-foot granite mansard, we had actually created a "lake" of tons of water standing more than thirty feet above the ground.

Their solution to this very dangerous problem was to place six large metal cylinders along the sidewalls, bail out the water, then drill a six-inch hole inside each of the cylinders through the decking. PVC pipe downspouts were then elbowed out through the brick walls and down to the ground.

I stood at some distance watching this process and

praying for success. When the metal cylinders were finally removed, I was amazed and relieved to see the water shooting out into the parking lot. In less than one hour, all of the water that had been "up there" was "down here."

Learning a Lesson from a Question

I knew that I was receiving another important lesson. The things in our life that we view as setbacks or misfortunes are often part of the sovereign purpose of God to provide spiritual instruction and growth.

When in my spirit I heard the question "Did the downspouts work?" I responded in the affirmative but heard the exact question again: "Did the downspouts work?" This happened three times and I finally said, "I am not sure at this point. Did the downspouts work?" The answer I received in my spirit was life changing: "The downspouts functioned, but they did not work— that is, they did not labor!"

From that amazing moment, I began to be aware of the relationship between the heavenly and earthly dimensions. The heavens are pregnant with purpose and power. All of our straining and trying has little effect.

We sometimes think God responds to us because we pray often or because we do good things for others. But the same rain that waters the gardens of faithful church-goers also waters the gardens of those who never cross the threshold of a church building.

> I began to be aware of the relationship between the heavenly and earthly dimensions.

God does not answer us because of our great effort but because we come into spiritual alignment with Him. If we are going to extend great energy, it should be to enter into His order or, as explained in chapter four of the Book of Hebrews, to enter into His rest. So instead of trying to convince God that we are worthy and that it would be a good idea to bless us with the answer to our requests, maybe we should seek the alignment that would cause His heavenly abundance to supply our earthly need.

Becoming God's Conduit

There was an abundance of water on the church roof but it had no way to be released onto the earth below. It actually crushed the roof of one building and was oozing out of small cracks in our ceiling. It reminds me of how much God desires to break forth in the earth and shower upon it blessings.

Our church roof needed a conduit or portal so that the water could reach the earth. The provision of God is like that. When it was finally released, the water had such great force that it shot out thirty feet from the end of the pipe. We need to learn to become the conduit, to give direction and structure to spiritual blessings.

When we come into proper spiritual order and alignment, God sovereignly manifests His will in our lives. "Thy kingdom come, Thy will be done in earth, as it is [already finished] in heaven" (Matthew 6:10). It is no longer about our effort. We simply become the vessels through which He manifests Himself in the earth.

Surprised by the Miraculous

I was surprised by the potential catastrophe of our church roof. I was relieved by the answer provided by the conduits. And I was in wonderful amazement, not only because God had spared us injury but because He made me wonder about what had happened, and in wondering He taught me some great lessons.

Through the following weeks, I ministered a series of messages that I titled "Surprised by the Miraculous." The theme was that God is not greatly impressed by our works. He simply requires that we come into agreement with His Word—the Word that is forever "settled [finished] in heaven" (Psalms 119:89). I even went so far as to say that when we come into agreement with His Word and prepare an atmosphere of faith, God will surprise us with the miraculous.

At the close of one of these meetings, I was approached by a lady who was obviously distraught. She had worn glasses from her childhood and was at this point almost legally blind. She often quipped, "Looking through these glasses is like looking through the bottom of two Coke bottles."

She tearfully explained that during the service, it had become impossible for her to see her Bible and that everything looked fuzzy and out of shape. She pleaded for me to pray that she would not lose what little sight she had left.

I looked at her for a moment, and then said, "Take off your glasses." She had been completely healed during the ministry of the word and her thick glasses, instead of helping her sight, were now blurring her vision. She, along with all of us, was surprised and amazed!

Insights into Spiritual Portals: Preparation and Timing

And a certain man lame from his mother's womb was carried, whom they laid daily at the gate of the temple which is called Beautiful, to ask alms of them that entered into the temple; Who seeing Peter and John about to go into the temple asked an alms. And Peter, fastening his eyes upon him with John, said, Look on

us. And he gave heed unto them, expecting to receive
something of them. Then Peter said, Silver and gold
have I none, but such as I have give I thee: In the name
of Jesus Christ of Nazareth rise up and walk. And he
took him by the right hand, and lifted him up: and
immediately his feet and ankle bones received strength.
And he leaping up stood, and walked, and entered
with them into the temple, walking, and leaping, and
praising God. (Acts 3:2–8)

Access to the miraculous is not a chance occurrence. It is prepared in advance for our benefit and for
divine purpose. The lame man in the story above was
carried to the Beautiful Gate every day so he could beg
for money. No doubt even
Jesus may have passed by
this individual during His
many visits to the temple.
Though Jesus healed all
who came to Him, He did
not make it a practice to seek out individuals to dis-
pense spiritual blessing to—this was not His primary
mission. For over forty years, this lame man was rele-

> Access to the
> miraculous is not a
> chance occurrence.

gated to a life of begging, until one day Peter and John walked by and he asked them for help. We can only give what we possess. Peter and John had no money to give this man, but they did have the Spirit of God and by that Spirit were able to heal him. The timing of God and the purpose of God intersected at that moment to open this heavenly portal of healing. Not only was this man restored to perfect health but this event served to confirm the words of Peter and John to those who witnessed this event.

Some things in your life require preparation. This man had a need that was over forty years old. This does not mean that we need to wait forty years to access the spiritual but that the timing and purpose of God are always involved in our access to spiritual portals. Understanding God's timing and purpose provides for us a great window into the miraculous. This type of understanding comes when you dare to believe in God for amazing things and prepare yourself to receive them.

Personal Application

Why do you suppose signs and wonders seem to happen to some people but not to others? I thought about this for a long time and I suppose there are many answers, but the more I thought about it, the more I realized that perhaps He does these things for everyone but not everyone has eyes to see what He is doing. Like the woman with the Coke-bottle glasses, the sight of some people is blurred by the things they allow to interfere with their spiritual vision.

The unusual fog that saved Washington's army by allowing it to retreat from Long Island right under the noses of the British is one such example. To the British army it was hardly a wonder sent by God. To many of the Continental soldiers, it was merely good fortune. But to Washington and a number who witnessed the deliverance, it was nothing short of a miracle and a wondrous act of God. They all experienced the same fog, but they had different responses.

Father, glorify thy name. Then came there a voice from heaven, saying, I have both glorified it, and will glorify it again. The people therefore, that stood by, and heard it, said that it thundered: others said, An angel spake to him. (John 12:28–29)

When this voice spoke from heaven, some said it must be thunder, others said an angel had spoken to Jesus, and at least one heard the words that were spoken. There were three different responses to the same supernatural event.

Wonders are miraculous events that cause us to wonder about God, His nature, and His ways of doing things. They happen to all of us, but not all perceive. They may know something has happened, but they chalk it up to a natural event: "It thundered." Others may recognize that something of a spiritual nature is happening but are not quite sure what it is: "An angel must have spoken to Him." While still others understand because they are in spiritual order to receive.

Pay attention! To heighten your sensitivity to spiritual things, look for the hand of God in all that happens in your life. Chance meetings, inconvenient phone calls, unexpected good or bad news, delays at airports, getting the last sale item at the store, and hundreds of other everyday events can be doorways to the wondrous workings of God.

> To heighten your sensitivity to spiritual things, look for the hand of God in all that happens in your life.

Do something with what you receive! Whenever a spiritual operation is in progress, all some people ever know is that "it thundered." When others in your department are being transferred or facing layoff but you have been spared, don't just say, "Thank you, God," but ask yourself, "Why? What is God's purpose in this? What is He trying to show me about Himself?"

Or if everyone in your department is keeping their job but you are being let go, don't say, "Woe is me," but search for His purpose and view the perceived setback for its potential benefit rather than from a position of fear. If God is in it, He is doing a wonder—not for your harm but for your benefit.

Remember! Remember the times God has done miraculous things in your life. The things we think about are the things that tend to happen. So meditate on the signs and wonders He has done in the scripture, for others, or for you. It will open up enormous possibilities and allow you to hear the voice from heaven.

Amaze us, O God, by the power of Your wonder!

CHAPTER THREE

Amazing Awakening

*The LORD God hath given me the tongue of the
learned, that I should know how to speak a word in
season to him that is weary: he wakeneth morning by
morning, he wakeneth mine ear to hear as the learned.*

—ISAIAH 50:4

*To awaken spiritually you must be shaken out of
the complacency of routine by learning to look at life
through the eyes of youth. Weary adults often question
so they don't have to embrace change but the young at
heart tend to question in order to believe and discover
more of life.*

—ROGER ROTH

I was awakened by the rising level of noise—music,
shouting, and stomping feet. From my limited van-

tage point beneath the old oak pew, my first thoughts were that someone needed to open the damper on the stove top. That's what my daddy did when the potbellied stove in the living room of the farmhouse started smoking.

The next thing I saw from my lowly perch was my mother's feet moving in a strange dancing motion, and I thought she must be trying to get someone's attention because the whole place was so smoky I could hardly see. I was four years old and during the extended "revival meetings" that continued night after night for weeks in the little "holiness church" in Newark, Ohio, my designated spot was a pallet on the floor under the pew, squarely behind my mother's feet.

If you have never been around what many call "old-time religion"—with its multitude of rules and regulations that are held on equally important par with the cross and empty tomb—my continued thoughts may make very little sense to you. This church was what many today would describe as a tongue-talking, scripture-thumping, Bible-toting, fundamentalist church.

I had a lot of time to study my mother's shoes. They didn't have holes in the toes like some of the worldly ladies wore. Having heard conversations between my mother and older sisters, I understood that ladies' shoes with holes in the toes were not holy.

It seemed to me that this was really wrong thinking. Everyone knows that the more holes shoes have, the "holier" they are. However, at this point, I really didn't care whose shoes were holier, and at that age I didn't really understand the "standards of holiness" or the various rules that accompanied that particular brand of Christianity.

I was concerned that the whole place was on fire and no one was aware of it. There was so much smoke that it looked to me like the whole building must be ablaze.

With a certain fear and childish curiosity, I crawled out from under the pew and watched in horror while my mother danced and twirled, with one arm raised high while the other loosely clutched my newborn baby sister.

There was so much smoke that it looked to me like the whole building must be ablaze.

I remember to this very day my sense of great relief

when one of the ladies rescued my sister, and only then did I realize that she and everyone around me was smiling and happy. They didn't seem to be at all concerned about the smoke. They were laughing, clapping, and singing as though something wonderful was happening, and then suddenly I realized that the smoke was gone.

My father, who was the pastor, explained to me on the way home late that night that what I had seen was not smoke. He said that the church building had an oil furnace that didn't smoke. "What you saw," he said, "was the glory cloud."

As I insisted on the smoke theory, he further explained that from time to time, God manifests His presence in various and unusual ways. He said that some people actually see the glory of God like a cloud and that others see angels and visions of all kinds.

He went on to say that the spirit world, where God and angels live, is real; but we only see it if we look for it and only experience it if we expect it. After sixty-four years, that amazing evening has been reinforced by many others and is still alive in my spirit and faithful to my daddy's word. I have continually sought to discover the miraculous in all things.

Beyond the Natural

In American history we use the term "The Great Awakening" to describe several periods of widespread revival and spiritual transformation. It is interesting that they occurred in the generation that preceded a great national struggle. The term "awakening" implies that people were spiritually asleep and needed to be awakened to God's very real presence and purpose. I would suggest that the awakening was a shift within the hearts of the people to search for the reality of God and His will above the everyday desires of life.

The First Great Awakening preceded the American Revolution, and even founding fathers such as Benjamin Franklin reported on its events and effect on the nation. The Second Great Awakening occurred roughly between 1800 and 1840 and had strong antislavery leanings, forging a path for change that came from the Civil War and its aftermath. The Third Great Awakening—the one during which my Aunt Ruth and grandmother were healed—prepared the nation for the very difficult and turbulent period of the World Wars and the Great Depression.

I mention this because I believe we as a nation and most probably as a world are on the verge of another Great Awakening. Our institutions have let us down and no hope or trust placed in political parties or in a man have provided an answer. In such times as these, like our forefathers, I believe we are once again seeking out the supernatural.

> *And the glory of the LORD shall be revealed, and all flesh shall see it together: for the mouth of the LORD hath spoken it.* (Isaiah 40:5)

With this search there is an element that is counterfeit and phony, lacking spiritual genuineness. This has always been the case as people begin to open their eyes to the spiritual dimension. As I awoke that day, in the small church in Newark, Ohio, to see the glory of God as a cloud of smoke, so I believe we are entering a time when many are awakening to the genuine spiritual possibilities in God.

It has always been interesting to me that some who believe in a God who is all-powerful—as well as in angels, heaven, and biblical miracles—have difficulty believing that this same God would manifest His power through signs and wonders in our day. Heaven is a real place and God's miraculous manifestation is available to the spiritually awake.

> Heaven is a real place and God's miraculous manifestation is available to the spiritually awake.

The miraculous is real, but we often need to be awakened to its nearness and its reality. Our dreams, whatever they may be, remain only dreams until they are in some way manifested in the earth.

Today my father's words, "The spirit world, where God and angels live, is real; but we only see it if we look for it and only experience it if we expect it," are more profound than when first spoken to me.

Insights into Spiritual Portals: Becoming Awakened

To look for and to expect are the actions that awaken us to the spiritual world.

*And Elijah came unto all the people, and said, How
long halt ye between two opinions? if the Lord be God,
follow him: but if Baal, then follow him. And the
people answered him not a word.* (1 Kings 18:21)

*And it came to pass in the mean while, that the heaven
was black with clouds and wind, and there was a great
rain.* (1 Kings 18:45)

The opening of portals always has a greater purpose than
the spiritual expression they release. The spiritual manifestation accompanying an open portal always points to
God and His greater purpose. So if God has provided for
you in some significant way, that blessing or miraculous
manifestation should also be accompanied by understanding, direction, and, most of all, a greater sense of
who and what God is to you.

The prophet Elijah ministered to Israel in a very
spiritually and politically turbulent time. Spiritual
expression had many outlets typified by religious expressions that were devoid of biblical truth. The people
were searching for spirituality in all the wrong places—
even through the false god Baal—and had forsaken

their earlier traditions. A great natural and spiritual drought came upon the land. Elijah, through a series of remarkable miracles, awakened Israel once again to spirituality. He renewed their expectation of God. After a national spiritual adjustment and upon Elijah's prayer, a heavenly portal was opened and it rained again after a three-and-one-half-year drought. The manifestation accompanying this portal was abundant rain, but the greater purpose of God was to restore Israel to spirituality. The Israelites were reawakened to the reality of God and an expectation of His presence.

Self-examination and expectation are keys that allow you to access the miraculous, like the people in Elijah's day, who had to be awakened to the reality of God. Doubt and fear block an expectant faith. We can use biblical examples and the divine manifestations given to others to stimulate our expectation that God will do likewise in our lives.

Personal Application

Each of us is awakened to certain things in God, and each of us is probably asleep to some things of the

Spirit until need or opportunity for our spiritual arousal presents itself. Divine pursuit and expectation awaken us to greater spiritual possibility.

> Divine pursuit and expectation awaken us to greater spiritual possibility.

What are you pursuing in God? Are you seeking an answer or some spiritual empowerment? You first must identify what you are pursuing. This will wake you up to look for how God is moving in your request.

Don't limit God by your preconceived ideas. Each of us, to one degree or another, has worked out in our mind what God is like and what He will or won't do. Part of awakening to the greater possibility of God is not to limit Him by your own limitations. Ask God to reveal Himself to you in new or varying ways and look for how He answers.

And most important, expect that He will answer. Expectation is a powerful spiritual tool. When we ask, He always answers—but not necessarily how we were thinking He would. We can have confidence that He will answer, but *how* he answers—in prayer, through people, by events, in some miraculous manifestation, etc.—is up to Him.

Our prayer, praise, and worship provide an atmosphere for His manifestation into our world. Their regular use are also great tools for your awakening.

Amaze us, O God, by Your power to awaken!

CHAPTER FOUR

Amazing Word

The word of God that is contained in the Bible has the power to do many marvelous things. Its most powerful attribute, perhaps, is its ability to mold God's nature in us so that we begin to see as He sees and think as He thinks and act as He acts. It molds us into His image and empowers us spiritually in our world!

—MARK HANDY

God's word is powerful. It formed the universe and everything in it, brought forth all life, and can reach down into the deepest part of our hearts to change despair into hope and want into fulfillment. It can give sight to physically blind eyes, and it gives sight to the spiritually blind as well. God is always speaking, and amazing things happen when we begin to distinguish His voice and act according to His direction.

I, as many of you, have personally experienced countless miraculous occurrences and have seen them unfold in the lives of others. I must admit that probably none of them were a consequence of anything I did but a result of something I found—spiritual portals in the heavens through which God acted and sovereignly dispensed His will. The key is to find out what God is up to and seek to participate in His will. One such portal that I witnessed was opened by a word that God had spoken.

Great Struggle Brings God's Intervention

For more than a dozen years, the red-and-white cane hung on the edge of the bookcase just inside my study door. Each time I passed it, I was reminded of that amazing evening when God miraculously healed the eyes of a man who was completely blind.

Through the years, I have come to understand that miraculous intervention most often occurs in times of great struggle. I suppose that is why we name our miracle by the crisis. Blindness, cancer, drug addiction, coma—all of these words become titles for divine deliverance.

As a church, we had grown and prospered to the point where we needed space and room for those we knew God

> Miraculous intervention most often occurs in times of great struggle.

was going to add to us. With excitement and the small amount of trepidation that accompany most undertakings of this magnitude, we decided to buy some land and build a new building.

This initial excitement turned into difficult days for me and for the weary congregation. Eighteen months of construction punctuated by some very serious setbacks had seemingly sucked the life and inspiration out of all of us. For example, the thirty-two-foot-high sidewalls were blown down one night during a North Texas wind, and the next morning our job superintendent decided to move to California. That was only the beginning of our woes.

By the time the beautiful new auditorium was completed, our well of joy was pretty much depleted. Our funds were gone, along with some prominent members who had vanished after informing the rest of us that we were out of the will of God and headed for certain failure. In their words, "No twenty-eight-year-old boy [meaning me] has the wisdom or ability for such a massive undertaking."

The most hurtful remarks, however, were whispered by fellow pastors in our fellowship who seemed joyous, even hopeful, for our failure. They concluded that I was simply trying to be a "big shot, buying all that land and building such a monstrosity," and was in way over my head.

In the years to come, we would eventually own 90 contiguous acres in the city, purchase 80 townhomes, and joint-venture 790 units of apartments—but all that would be after the following amazing miracle.

The truth is, I really wasn't trying to compete with anyone. I was tender, sensitive, and passionate for the kingdom. I spent many nights alone in that vast, dark auditorium contemplating the words of the naysayers with devastating effect. My inspiration and confidence were at an all-time low.

In our old building, with chairs in every aisle and

people standing in the foyer, one "hallelujah" would send the fresh young congregation into a bonfire of praise, while here in the new building, an "amen" sounded like the echo of a hoarse goat herder deep in the Swiss Alps. With row after row of pews roped off during services, we looked like a few lonely ducks on the Atlantic Ocean.

God Gives an Amazing Word

Late one night after every one had gone home from the evening service, I sat once again in the dark auditorium. My thoughts and prayers were interrupted by a powerful presence, and I heard what I knew to be the voice of the Lord. He spoke an amazing word to me: "I am going to do notable miracles in this place!" The words

I heard what I knew to be the voice of the Lord.

ripped through my depression like a razor-sharp sword. Faith exploded in my spirit, and I vaulted off the platform, shouting with holy anticipation.

For weeks after, I boldly announced that God was going to do notable miracles in this place. After a while, I could feel a certain skepticism in some, while others made an effort to believe.

It happened at the end of our midweek Bible study. In closing, I once again reminded the folks of the word I had heard from the Lord. One of my precocious parishioners stood up and began pulling a rather frail-looking fellow toward the aisle. "My friend," she loudly announced, "needs a notable miracle." She led him forward with that red-and-white cane waving in front of his feet.

I was somewhat taken aback or, should I say, placed squarely on the spot. Since I wasn't quite sure how to handle this rather uncomfortable situation, I decided that a little conversation couldn't hurt. I asked his name, he told me, and then he launched into an entire history of his life.

I shifted from foot to foot while Clem explained that he had worked at the county courthouse as a courier for most of his adult life and that they had "kindly kept him on" after the retinas of his eyes had peeled away. "Can't see light or dark, no shadows . . . nothing," he explained. "I can still move around the courthouse better than those kids. All the judges and attorneys down there like me. We've been knowin' each other for years."

I decided it was time to intervene. "How long have you been blind?" I asked. He answered, "I have been totally blind for fourteen years. Kinda get used to it after a while."

Reaching for a little faith, I asked the next question. "Clem, do you believe Jesus can open your eyes?" and he answered without hesitation, "I don't know."

I suppose I should have been stunned, but I was immediately embraced by the same inspiration that had spoken to me in weeks earlier about the coming of notable miracles. Without forethought, I began speaking words to him that came directly into my spirit. "Do you believe that if Jesus were actually here He could open your eyes?" His eyes looked like two yellowish marbles as he vacantly stared toward me and answered, "Oh yes, I believe that!"

The next words that flowed out of my mouth came with a powerful anointing. "Please don't be surprised, Clem, but when I walked over here to you, He came with me, and He is here beside me right now!" He shifted his cane and reached out his right hand as though to touch this unseen Christ. I watched in wonder as the milky film seemed to drain from his eyes and he screamed, "I can see!"

> I watched in wonder as the milky film seemed to drain from his eyes.

The next day, the front page of a local newspaper ran an article that read, "Well-known county employee blind for 14 years claims to be healed through the power of prayer." The article went on to say, "The county courthouse was in an uproar this morning."

My message the following Sunday was "We have toiled all the night, and have taken nothing: nevertheless at thy word I will let down the net" (Luke 5:5). The church was packed with people in the aisles and out into the foyer. It was like an unstopped well that refreshed us and carried us to amazing new places in the Spirit.

By the way, after that event we never had to put ropes on the pews again.

Insights into Spiritual Portals:
The Power of the Word

> *He sent his word, and healed them, and delivered them from their destructions.* (Psalms 107:20)

> *When the even was come, they brought unto him many that were possessed with devils: and he cast out the spirits with his word, and healed all that were sick.* (Matthew 8:16)

Words are perhaps the most powerful tool we humans possess. A few well-placed words with evil intent can shake most individuals and destroy their confidence, or if spoken in truth and kindness, uplift a broken spirit. The Bible is often called the Word of God. God's words have both natural and supernatural power.

God is speaking to each of us, and He often speaks to us through words He places within people willing to speak those words. I have witnessed hope restored, bodies healed, and seemingly insurmountable circumstances overcome because people were willing to speak the words God has given them. Sometimes individuals speak their own words as though they came from God, to no effect. But if He gives you words and you speak them with confidence, then God's miraculous power will come to any situation. The surest way to become sensitized to hear His words is to give attention to His Word. In reading and meditating on Scripture the entire miraculous power of His Word becomes available to you to accomplish His purpose.

Personal Application

Some of you feel like the apostles: "Lord, we toiled and worked all night and have caught nothing." This spiritual journey is wearing you out, and you need some rest and a fresh word from God.

When God gives a word, it will come to pass; but we have to be open to His will by becoming willing participants. What would have happened if the apostles had said, "Lord, we have toiled all night without any result, so, even though you are asking us to, we are not going to fish anymore today"? The likely outcome is that they would have missed out on the miracle.

God has told some of us amazing things. He really

said them to us. Faith is exercised by not only believing what God said but also acting on it.

Recount the things God has told you. In the Scripture we are often instructed to remember. In remembering what He has said to us at other times, we open ourselves to His voice and to hearing His current word for us.

It is in our struggle that we often receive His greatest word—as we did at Truth Church when His Word answered our need and revealed to us once again His great love and power. Revisit some of your struggles to recall God's intervention and faithfulness.

Sometimes we go through things without God. Not because He is unavailable or unwilling to do good on our behalf, but because we sometimes close ourselves to spiritual possibilities and try to work things out solely in our human effort. Perhaps you have gone through or now are going through such an event. Try looking at your situation through the eyes of God and adjusting your thinking according to a fresh perception.

Amaze us, O God, by the power of Your Word!

CHAPTER FIVE

Amazing Belief

You've heard it said that "some things have to be seen to be believed." Well, with God, some things have to be believed in order to be seen. Some people's minds are closed by what they believe; others' minds are opened by daring to believe what most would reject.

Everyone believes in something, but what they believe in determines what they receive. When a word from God has been confirmed to you, hang on to it and don't let go, for God's word always produces the result He intends.

—MARK HANBY

The year was 1973, and I was conducting a Christian crusade in the Philippines. The meetings were being held in the large boxing arena on the Manila harbor. This is the same facility where the "Thrilla in

Manila" between Muhammad Ali and the late Joe Frazier took place. Two hundred fifty national pastors had been gathered from the various islands to assist, and the city had been well-saturated with various forms of advertising.

Since the Philippine Islands were a United States territory before World War II, most of the people understood English, and therefore, I did not have to speak through an interpreter. I had also been told that previous crusades had been well attended but that the ministries had met with only limited spiritual response due to the warnings and control of the city's entrenched religious establishment. They permitted attendance but not participation.

The first two nights proceeded with only limited reception. Although the arena was packed, very few answered the offer of prayer or spiritual impartation.

I spent the daytimes alone in prayer asking the Lord to give me the words to change the minds and hearts of the people. The third evening, I ministered from Mark chapter 9, verse 24. I used the words spoken by the father of a demon-possessed child, "Lord, I believe; help thou mine unbelief," as the basis for my talk.

As I told the story, I continued to repeat, "Lord, I believe," stressing the importance of personal faith—"You must say, 'Lord, I believe,'" I repeated. "We may not understand all things, but a willingness to believe opens up great divine potential."

> A willingness to believe opens up great divine potential.

Then something totally unexpected happened. I had an overwhelming sense that God was about to intervene and give a sign to the people. As I continued my message, I sought in my spirit to interpret the sense that was upon me. As I yielded to the strong urging of the Spirit, I knew I was to speak. Without forethought, these words came out of my mouth, "The lights in this great auditorium are about to go out. Please do not panic. It is a sign from God."

There was no storm, the weather was balmy, and I had no knowledgeable reason to say those words; but as soon as I had spoken, every light in the arena went out! I stood still in the darkness. The microphone had no power. I could not continue ministering and I was aware of the very dangerous possibility of crowd panic.

Very quietly at first, then louder and louder, the people in the arena began to chant: "I believe . . . I believe . . . I believe . . ." The people were becoming spiritually awakened to the divine presence that was sweeping over that arena. Their chanting reached a powerful crescendo, and the whole auditorium was alive with faith.

While this continued, men whom we did not know began coming out of the streets carrying bottles with fluid and cloth wicks. They lit them and stood around the staging area. Without a microphone but with a fresh and powerful anointing, I proclaimed to the people that the God who controls the light and the darkness has the power to heal and deliver—nothing is impossible to those who believe.

The people began chanting again, "I believe . . . I believe . . ." and then the lights came on. Without invitation the people surged forward. Miracles were happening all around me. People were throwing canes and crutches in a pile in front of the stage. Parents were setting crippled children onto their feet. The whole place was in a holy uproar!

The national pastors worked their way through the

crowd as hundreds were being baptized in the Spirit. They later reported many of the outstanding miracles they had witnessed. One twelve-year-old girl, born crippled, not only walked but was running in the aisles of the auditorium. Four blind people they knew of were healed, one of whom was a nineteen-year-old young man who had been born blind.

It was impossible to preach in the following services. The people literally chanted for hours, "I believe!" while untold numbers of miracles took place. I simply became a bystander beholding the wonderful works of God. The missionaries later informed me that the spiritual wave continued in various parts of the city for months following the crusade.

Help My Unbelief

When I returned home, I stood before my congregation and recited many of the things that had happened. My excitement was not met with a sense of wonder and joyful response. I had envisioned them being overcome with faith and praise. Somehow the events seemed too good to be true. Though they had witnessed a multitude of miracles personally, they had not witnessed the events in Manila, and therefore, it did not affect them the same way.

I closed the service without ministering and urged everyone to go home. I then lay prostrate behind the pulpit and wept for the unbelief of the American church. Even today most of the church have not realized what they are missing of God because they have closed themselves to divine manifestation by their unbelief.

I do not mean to sound judgmental or cruel. After all my years of ministering to this Christian nation, I am still aware that, though real and completely true, these accounts seem far removed from our modern brand of production religion.

Someone, please, turn the lights back on!

Faith Triggers

Jesus saith unto him, Thomas, because thou hast seen me, thou hast believed: blessed are they that have not seen, and yet have believed. (John 20:29)

There are things that trigger our faith. In Manila the word of knowledge about the lights going out was a definite sign that triggered the faith of those gathered. Once set in motion, the fruit of their faith continued for months—but what did it trigger them to do? It initiated a belief in the spoken Word of God: "Lord, I believe; help thou mine unbelief."

We can believe many things, but genuine faith must be generated by God and His word to us. Thomas believed Jesus rose again because he could physically see the nail prints in his hands and feet. Many of us have been conditioned by spiritual complacency to only believe something we can physically see and touch.

> Genuine faith must be generated by God and His word to us.

Jesus said that those who have not seen and yet believe are blessed. We who are alive today are blessed because we have believed in Jesus without physically seeing Him. If we can believe in Jesus, whom we have not seen, why should we not also believe in His miraculous power and His manifestation in our dimension?

Believing God

What we believe is different from our *capacity* for believing. Humans have a great capacity for believing all kinds of things. We can make ourselves believe someone loves us when they don't and that someone doesn't love us when in fact they do. Some believe things that are met with skepticism by most—Martians from outer space, get-rich-quick schemes, outlandish conspiracy theories—a whole gamut of fringe ideas. Others only believe what they can see and touch and confirm.

As indicated above, belief falls into two broad general categories: first is belief in things substantiated by what we consider fact; second is belief in things generated by our imagination or the imaginations of others. Believing God falls into an entirely different category we call faith. It is a spiritual operation that is substantiated by fact. What we hear from God and see in the heavens becomes reality in our earth.

Insights into Spiritual Portals: Spiritual Manifestations

> But the manifestation of the Spirit is given to every man to profit withal. For to one is given by the Spirit the word of wisdom; to another the word of knowledge by the same Spirit; To another faith by the same Spirit; to another the gifts of healing by the same Spirit; To another the working of miracles; to another prophecy; to another discerning of spirits; to another divers kinds of tongues; to another the interpretation of tongues: But all these worketh that one and the selfsame Spirit, dividing to every man severally as he will. (1 Corinthians 12:7–11)

God had given me a word of knowledge for those gathered in that Manila arena. That word coupled with God's demonstration ignited the faith of those gathered so that great manifestations of His power and love were witnessed.

God manifests Himself in many ways. The manifestation of His Spirit in the earth comes in at least nine significant ways—as seen in the passage quoted above. He tells us that these manifestations are given to every person, which means that all who have a relationship with the Spirit of God have access to them. By understanding the operation of these nine spiritual manifestations and understanding their use, each individual can participate in bringing forth His miraculous power.

> Each individual can participate in bringing forth His miraculous power.

"But covet earnestly the best gifts: and yet shew I unto you a more excellent way" (1 Corinthians 12:31). We are told to fervently desire the best gifts (the best gifts as they pertain to His purpose for us individually), and yet there is an ultimate method to walking in this miraculous empowerment, and that way, as Paul goes on to describe, is love.

Love will open to you the power of the Spirit because God's very essence is love. Love will always act right, think right, and do right. Love never makes a mistake. To learn and to grow in love is to learn and grow in God and, in so doing, to receive access to spiritual power.

Personal Application

When the father of the boy who was possessed came to Jesus in Mark 9, he pleaded with Jesus to "have compassion on us, and help us." Jesus didn't say, "Okay, I'll do it," but told him, "If thou canst believe, all things are possible to him that believeth." Our belief is a requirement of God's action.

The man said to Jesus, "I believe; help thou mine unbelief." Isn't this how we often feel? We believe that God can do it, we just don't know if He will do it or how He will do it.

Some of what is called worship is little more than performance religion. It is more like a musical presentation than anything centered in heartfelt praise. Genuine worship is a wonderful way to increase our ability to believe. Centering our worship on something God has promised or something He has spoken increases our capacity to place our faith in Him.

> Genuine worship is a wonderful way to increase our ability to believe.

Recounting miraculous events in your life can also

generate faith. The power of personal testimonies cannot be overrated in their ability to bring the reality of God into our daily lives.

Meditating on specific scriptures also can help us entertain divine possibilities. The Word is powerful and alive and brings life to our spiritual desires.

Amaze us, O God, by the power of belief!

CHAPTER SIX

Amazing Trust

Can we truly trust God with our eternal destiny if we cannot trust Him with our daily lives? We don't always trust God because we are not sure whether His will for us is the same as our will for ourselves.

—ROGER ROTH

There is often a fine line between trusting God and trusting something we think is God. Many years ago, I was told a story by a missionary friend that I believe demonstrates amazing trust, and I want to share it with you.

Mother Freeman had been widowed for several years but was comforted by her two young sons, whom she loved dearly. She spent a great deal of time teaching the boys the ways of God and watched them grow up to be fine young men. One of them, the friend who shared this story with me, felt a call to the ministry and eventually left home to fulfill his call in a foreign mission field. The other son was drafted into the armed forces and was sent overseas during World War Two.

Christian friends who knew Mother Freeman testified that she spent most of her time praying for her beloved sons, who were now both far away. She continued to laden the mail carrier with letters of encouragement, assuring both sons that God had promised her that they would one day return safely.

Eventually the missionary son did return home and accepted the pastorate of a small congregation near his mother's home in southern Louisiana, but the younger son remained at war. It had been several weeks and then months since she had received any return correspondence or word from her son on the front line.

Then came that awful day when an army representative knocked on her door holding a large manila envelope with a few personal items and an official letter from the commander in chief. With deep apology and obvious sympathy, he drew out the letter and began to read.

When the messenger got to the words "missing in action and presumed dead," Mother Freeman interrupted him, and without a tear or any outward demonstration of emotion said, "John is not dead!" She went on to say, "You can take your envelope and letter back to the president and tell him what I said. John is not dead."

Her ministry son went on to tell me that friends and family members all eventually accepted his brother's death. "All except Mom. She continued to declare that while she had no idea where he was, John would come home." He went on to say that the family had simply concluded that the years of loneliness and emotional grief had affected his mother's mind and that she had, in many ways, lost touch with reality.

When they pressed her, she would simply say, "God made me a promise, and I trust Him." Mother Freeman watched the road by day and by night sat in her rocker facing the front door. When folks came by, urging her to go to bed, she would often just ask them to hand her a throw and would sleep in her chair facing the door.

"God made me a promise, and I trust Him."

Five years went by, and then they stretched to ten

long years, as this aging mother continued to wait for the promise of God. She never left her watch—"God promised, and I trust Him." Late one night fifteen years after the messenger of death had knocked on her door, there came another knock. Mother Freeman struggled out of her rocker.

When she opened the door, there stood a frail, bearded man, obviously malnourished and ill. She looked at him for a moment, then said, "Where have you been, John? I have been waiting for you for fifteen years!" War, prison camps, and John's inability to cope had taken him away; but a promise from God and a mother's amazing trust had brought him home.

The Loss of Trust

We all trust in something. Even people who say they don't trust anyone or anything are putting trust in their opinion that nothing is to be trusted. People who trust only in themselves are typically lonely and emotionally isolated.

Trusting others is an exercise in faith, but trusting

only in yourself is a result of fear. As a society, our growing sense of isolation is a consequence of lost confidence in our institutions and in each other.

In our present world, trust and faith are becoming precious commodities. The ultimate source of all trust, like love, is found in God. This is why the farther our society strays from a desire for God and the miraculous, the less it will be able to trust.

A recent Gallup Poll (June 9–11, 2011) confirmed what many already realize: trust in most institutions is at an all-time low. The survey revealed that virtually every institution has lost public trust. Results from this poll showed that less than half trust organized religion, the medical system, or public schools. Less than a third trust the media, banks, labor unions, big business, or Congress.

Born to Trust

Faith is not belief without proof, but trust without reservation.

—DAVID ELTON TRUEBLOOD

It is natural to trust. Part of innocence is a willingness to trust those who speak into our lives. Children are often called gullible because they tend to believe without reservation things told them by those in authority. This is even true when evidence around them seems to contradict the thing they are trusting.

Think of Santa Claus. The only reason the young believe in this benevolent gift-giver is that they are told to and given manufactured evidence in the form of gifts from Santa on Christmas, supplying proof that he exists.

Like Santa, almost everything in a child's life is taken on faith. "Listen to me—I know better. Don't eat that, it will make you sick. Grandma loves you; don't talk to strangers; God doesn't like it when you do that" are only a very few of the things children believe when told to do so by someone they trust.

Trained to Distrust

We have to be taught not to trust. As humans we want to trust. We want to have faith in each other. But in reality, we don't have a childlike faith and trust because people and events have continually betrayed that trust.

As humans we want to trust. We want to have faith in each other.

Most desire the benefits derived from trusting, but many do not understand the nature of trust or the attitudes required to make it possible. To trust in anything or anyone besides God, we have to accept the possibility that we may be disappointed or even defrauded.

Trust encompasses risk, vulnerability, and the possibility of betrayal. For these reasons, among humans, trust is almost always conditional. We often say of people who have violated our trust, "I'll never trust that person again," or "If they want my trust, from now on they will have to earn it."

What we are saying is that these people will have to provide evidence worthy of our trust. This is a reasonable response, but it is also the response of conditional trust. Trust carries with it the sense of the unknown, but it is the seedbed of our future triumphs.

Faith Working with Trust

Trust always involves faith. Without faith there can be no trust, and without trust we limit faith. We could say that our amount of trust is conditioned on the level of our faith.

Faith, trust, and belief are all interconnected terms, but there are important distinctions. For example, we can believe God for things He has promised or spoken, but faith requires our belief plus our action. This is why the Bible tells us that faith without works (or faith without some corresponding action) is dead. Jesus told the disciples in Mark 11:22 not to have faith for things or for miracles but to "have faith in God." He needs to be the focus of our faith. Consider the scripture in Matthew 17:19–20. The disciples want to know why they could not cast out a certain demon and Jesus tells them, "Because of your unbelief; for verily I say unto you, if ye have faith as a grain of mustard seed, ye shall say to this mountain, Remove hence to yonder place; and it shall remove; and nothing shall be impossible unto you."

With faith you can increase faith, lack faith, grow in

faith, and so forth, but you can't have unfaith. Romans
12:3 tells us that God has given each person a "measure
of faith." Faith comes from God and is acted on by us.
God does not give us belief in the same sense He gives
us faith. A person can believe or not believe; it is a response from us toward God. If we choose not to use or
don't understand how to use the faith given us, we can
walk, as the disciples did, in unbelief. The response to
faith is belief; the response to disregarding faith is unbelief. Trust is both a consequence of faith and a response
of believing. Our faith causes us to trust God and our
willingness to believe is a demonstration of our trust.

Belief is more a measure of trust than a measure of
faith. Faith is not merely believing. People believe all
kinds of strange things contrary to evidence. Faith is the
evidence of things that exist in the heavenly dimension
but that have not been seen or come to pass in the earth.
This heavenly evidence is supplied to us in a number of
ways: by hearing the voice of the Spirit, through signs
and wonders, by strange coincidences, through the
inspiration of the word of God, and in many other supernatural ways.

In faith we know and perceive the goodness of God

and that He is able, and because of this knowledge, we then act in a manner to bring His heavenly purpose to pass in the earth. Though there are measures of faith, faith is something we either use or disregard.

In having trust, I know that God is able, but there are things I may not know or understand. So my faith in God allows me to trust Him, according to what He has told me, even in those situations where I struggle to find understanding or answers.

Trust in God is the greatest demonstration of my faith. Even though I may not understand, I know that He loves me and that He is working His purpose out for my good—perhaps even something greater than the answer I am seeking.

Trust allows God to be God. It says that even in my distress and discomfort, God knows some things I do not know; and since I trust that His love for me is greater than my understanding, I submit my will to His.

Since I trust that His love for me is greater than my understanding, I submit my will to His.

God Sometimes Amazes Us by What He Does Not Do

I was a pastor for twelve years in Fort Worth before I preached my first funeral at the church. Considering that the size of the church at that time was over 2,500 members, that is an amazing thing. When we had our first death, I remember how it shook the congregation. This was something we were not used to, and it occurred when great signs and wonders were taking place.

What really shook the congregation was that the person who died was not an elderly member but a vibrant woman in her forties who had cancer. Naomi was one of the sweetest women. She was a person of faith and someone who was esteemed as a perfect example of what it meant to be Christlike.

Everyone prayed for her and expected her to be healed. And why not? With all the amazing things that were happening day after day, her healing would be just one more example and testimony of God's power. But she continually grew weaker until she died.

It shook the church. Why did God let this happen,

especially to someone as wonderful as Naomi? When I preached her funeral, I spoke from the portion of Scripture that says, "Be thou faithful unto death, and I will give thee a crown of life" (Revelation 2:10).

Naomi was faithful to God even to the point of death. Death did not alter her attitude or faith in God. Death did not change her godly nature or her trust in Him.

Sometimes what we think to be great loss or the work of the enemy is really the hand of God. We trust Him when He unleashes fantastic miracles, but do we have the same trust when in His purpose and according to what He knows is best, His answer is contrary to our desire?

Naomi's death was actually a great lesson for the whole church in how to trust God. She demonstrated by her faithfulness, love, and trust of God that sometimes God can be even more amazing by not giving us what we desire but by answering our trust in Him. Naomi taught us to give God permission to be God.

Our Faith and Trust, Not Our Goodness, Connect Us to God's Power

We can have miracles and prosperity, but at some point—unless God restores the fullness of His Kingdom in our lifetime—we will die. The key is to be faithful, to be in a place of faith—to find a trust that goes deeper than our material desires. We think our goodness or righteousness is what moves God to do amazing things. I don't believe that is true. I've seen too many godly people die and too many good people suffer loss. I believe what moves God is our faith and trust in Him.

> What moves God is our faith and trust in Him.

It's like the story a pastor from Toronto, Canada, told me a long time ago. At the end of one of his services he was praying for people to be healed. A woman who had severely and permanently injured her arm in a bar fight was present and came up for prayer. She was not what you'd consider an example of femininity—her speech, her clothing, her reputation, and the way she carried herself all told of a woman who was rough and tough and able to hold her own in any scuffle.

When the invitation for prayer was given, she came forward. She had faith that she would be healed. God instantly healed her damaged limb, and it was restored to full use. Though God healed her body, she did not change her spiritual direction. She continued in the rough and rowdy lifestyle of excessive drinking and regular fracases.

Somewhat perplexed, the pastor said, "She came up for prayer and God healed her. Now she's a better brawler than before!"

Jesus healed multitudes of people. We sometimes think they were all worthy and well-deserving people—according to our understanding of worthiness. But how many—like the Canaanite woman in Matthew 15 who had a demon-possessed daughter—were healed not because of their righteousness but because of their faith?

Sometimes God amazes us by the things He does not do. How many times have you said, "I asked God for this or that and now I am glad He did not answer me according to my desire"?

Trust gives God permission to be God, to do whatever He knows is best for your life. Amazing things are not just things of deliverance. Sometimes He amazes us by the things He does not do.

Insights into Spiritual Portals: The Power of Faith

> *Jesus said unto him, If thou canst believe, all things are possible to him that believeth.* (Mark 9:23)

Today and every day, people and situations will enter your life to test and increase your faith. What you believe matters. If you can believe what God has said to you instead of those voices that stand opposed to God, then everything He tells you will be possible.

So when these situations occur, step back and understand them as an opportunity to increase your faith. Then you will see these events in an entirely different light and in so doing open up for yourself great spiritual opportunities.

Personal Application

LEARN TO TRUST UNCONDITIONALLY

Some of you may have been hurt by trusting people too much, but in actuality, the greater harm comes to those who don't trust enough. It is true that those you trust the most can also take the most from you. But trust is a measure of your willingness to love, and that is why great love always involves great trust.

So unless we can learn to trust God and to trust Him fully, we will always be conditional in our love for others, for ourselves, and for Him. Our trust is greater evidence of our love than our words. Trusting makes us vulnerable, but it also allows us to find love and contentment.

Is God worthy of your trust? Most of us would probably say yes, but then why do we not trust Him fully? Only unconditional trust can bring the realization of His unconditional love.

Scripture tells us to "Trust in the LORD with all thine heart" (Proverbs 3:5). Trust is primarily produced in the heart and not the mind. We all have been let down by people and have let others down as well. There is plenty of evidence in this world that people are not to be trusted.

Though we all have been given the insight and common sense not to allow others to freely abuse us, the tendency of our adult minds is to trust no one. This, taken to extremes, can become an emotional prison of our own making.

How are we to regain genuine trust in mankind, when people, institutions, and even some close to us have continually violated our trust and given us no reason to renew our confidence? How do we renew the vibrant trust and accep- tance of childhood in an atmosphere of wisdom and com- mon sense?

It begins with learning to trust that which cannot violate our trust. In my experience, the only one who meets this criterion is God. Though the actions of people may warrant conditional trust, God gives us reason to trust Him unconditionally.

> How do we renew the vibrant trust and acceptance of childhood in an atmosphere of wisdom and common sense?

Understand the Reward of Trust

*Trust in the Lord with all thine heart; and lean not
unto thine own understanding. In all thy ways
acknowledge him, and he shall direct thy paths.*
(Proverbs 3:5–6)

It is innate within man to trust God. The lack of trust
developed as a consequence of our human experience
often carries over to a lack of trust in God. The scripture
tells us not to trust in men or in riches but to "trust in
the LORD" and to do it with all our hearts. This is not a
mental exercise but a heart exercise.

We are not to lean on our own understanding; that
is, we are not to trust in what we see or experience, but
are to trust what we know in our hearts about God.
Trusting God will cause us to recognize Him in everything we think and do; and as a result, He will give
direction to the paths of our lives.

Confidence comes from having faith in God for
what you are doing. Consciously give God permission
to be God by coming to the place where no matter how
uncomfortable or hesitant you may be, you say to God,

"You know best, do your will even if it may not be what I presently desire."

If you cannot trust God, you will never be fully confident in yourself. Everyone trusts something, even if it is only their own opinion. The key to trust is not *what* you trust but *who* you trust in.

Amaze us, O God, by the power of trust!

CHAPTER SEVEN

Amazing Hope

Hope is the timeless desire to reconnect to the perfection of God; to have all things in your life align themselves to the eternal purpose of God so that your life can have ultimate meaning and significance. Hope makes today's dreams tomorrow's reality.

—ROGER ROTH

I t was one of those glorious services. I stood on the platform watching various manifestations of the Spirit. To many denominational church members, the whole affair would probably have been considered emotional hysteria. I was not greatly concerned, however, with the opinion of our religious critics.

I had spent a great deal of time explaining to the congregation that enthusiasm—*en-theosism*—means "the God of you." In other words, the thing that excites you the most is actually your god! The people loved the freedom of spiritual expression, and the whole place looked as though someone had scored a touchdown in the prayer meeting.

Standing toward the back of the auditorium was a couple whom I had been told desperately wanted children. They were in their mid-thirties and were considering adoption since they had no children of their own.

Caught up in the wave of faith, I motioned for them to come forward. As they approached the platform, I quieted the congregation and spoke into the microphone. I suppose that what I said could be considered prophetic; but to me in that moment, it was simply a statement of what I knew to be true without doubt.

"I understand that you are considering adopting a child, and I think that is noble; but I just need to tell you that God is going to bless you with a baby of your own!" The sweet couple looked stunned as I repeated, "God is going to give you a baby."

Rather than sharing my faith and excitement, the lady shook her head in a side to side movement and motioned me toward her. "Pastor," she whispered, "I have had a complete hysterectomy, and there is no way

I could possibly have a child." Now it was my turn to be shocked. I considered her words for a moment and replied, "I still believe what God says, regardless of the circumstances." She answered, "All right, Pastor, I am going to place my hope in God."

This dialogue had rather dampened the excitement in the house, and I eventually went off to my study feeling rather sheepish and embarrassed. Less than one year later, just as God had promised, she gave birth to a healthy baby boy. During his dedication service, she held her baby in one arm and her medical records in the other as the father explained the amazing miracle.

More than twenty years later, I was speaking in a local church on the East Coast. I noticed a middle-aged couple enter the building during my message and felt I should have recognized them. Their faces seemed strangely familiar. After the service, the couple approached me and handed me a picture of a handsome young man in a graduation gown. "Hi, Pastor. Thought you might like to see what he looks like now."

I knew them. These were the brave folks who had, like Abraham, "against hope believed in hope"! (Romans 4:18). Through the years, I have shared this story with some who frankly find it impossible to believe. I understand, but I also know that if it had been possible, it would not have been supernatural.

> If it had been possible, it would not have been supernatural.

Perhaps this, among other things, is what makes the birth of Jesus so amazing. In order for impossible things to come to pass in your life, they must be centered in hope.

The God Kind of Hope

The word *hope*, as applied by many, is equated with wishful thinking. When people say they have hope, what they usually mean is that they would like to see something good happen but are not sure it will. When they hope for good fortune in some area of their lives, they are expressing a wish or an uncertain optimism that what they are looking for will come to pass.

Hope, the God kind of hope, is not given to chance or probability. Hope is a powerful spiritual force. The God kind of hope comes with certainty; it is a confident expectation that what God said will come to pass.

I think a useful definition of what hope is could be summed up as follows: *Hope is a divine desire with patient anticipation and expectation that what God has promised will come to pass.* If hope involves a divine expectation, then it must be based on something God has told you or affirmed to you. When God says something will happen, you can have hope, because your desire and expectation *will* come to pass. It is not a question of probability but of certainty. This kind of hope is always fulfilled.

The difference between wishful thinking and godly hope is found in the *source* of your expectation. Hoping to become a concert pianist or find a buried treasure or marry the person of your dreams may only be wishful thinking unless the source of your desire is found in God.

The source of Abraham's hope was God:

(As it is written, I have made thee a father of many nations,) before him whom he believed, even God, who quickeneth the dead, and calleth those things which be not as though they were. Who against hope believed in hope, that he might become the father of many

nations, according to that which was spoken, So shall thy seed be. (Romans 4:17–18)

The hope that Abraham carried took many years to come to pass. Sarah gave Abraham the son of God's promise when he was one hundred years old. God's promise took a quarter of a century to come to pass, yet it did come to pass, because Abraham continued in hope.

That does not mean he walked in perfect understanding. The strength of hope is that it works even when we lack understanding or are overcome by frustration or moments of weakness.

The Process of Hope

There is a process to hope. "And not only so, but we glory in tribulations also: knowing that tribulation worketh patience; And patience, experience; and experience, hope" (Romans 5:3–4).

First, when God gives us a promise, the promise usually requires our participation through hope to bring it to pass. Then, He tests our desire and our motivation so that they are in line with His will. He does this so that we can test our motivation to see if our desire is a result of fear or selfishness rather than a desire for His will. Finally, He packages the focus of our hope in amazing circumstances so that we and others are convinced that the revealed promise is from Him.

This is what He did with Abraham. Abraham had the promise of a son from God, but after waiting years for it to come to pass, he tried to work out God's promise. First he thought to give to his servant the rights of a son. Then he had a son with his wife Sarah's maidservant. Both those events were attempts on Abraham's part to work out the long-awaited answer to the hope of Abraham for the son God had promised him. Finally, after a process of many years, Abraham received his promised son.

Abraham "against hope believed in hope, that he might become the father of many nations." When your wife is ninety years old and you still have hope that God's promise of a son through her is going to happen—even though she is long past the age of child-bearing—we could say that it is a perfect illustration of the phrase "who against hope believed in hope." Hope totally disregards your present circumstance and rests wholly in your faith and patience.

> Hope totally disregards your present circumstance and rests wholly in your faith and patience.

Have you ever tried to help God out with an expected promise rather than wait with patience for what He has told you will come to pass? I think we all have done this. This does not mean we lack faith, but it probably means we lack understanding. The things transferred from His Spirit to ours are eternal, and hope provides a continual spiritual link until what is in the heavenly dimension materializes in the earth.

The Linking of Faith and Hope

Now faith is the substance of things hoped for, the evidence of things not seen. (Hebrews 11:1)

Hope, in one sense, is greater than faith. Without faith it is impossible to please God, but we could also say that without hope it is impossible to have faith. Faith provides the substance in our material world of the hoped-for promises of God from heaven. Faith and hope always work together.

We are often told to have faith, or hope, for *things*. This, I believe, is an imperfect understanding and the cause of much of our confusion and discouragement. The scripture does not tell us to have faith for things but rather to have faith in God and hope in what He has promised—not hope for what we want irrespective of His promises.

When our hope or faith is focused on things, we are looking at the desired gift rather than at the giver. I believe this is what Abraham did. He was so focused on having a son that he took his eyes off the one who gave the promise and off the reason why He gave the promise and could only give place to his desperation and longing for a son. Focusing only on our desire will generate frustration, impatience, and mistakes; while focusing on God and His promises will lead to patient acceptance and anticipation.

Hope deferred maketh the heart sick: but when the desire cometh, it is a tree of life. (Proverbs 13:12)

One reason it is important to keep your eyes on God is that there is always a timing to the fulfillment of God's promises. God promised Israel a Messiah, but it was only when the fullness of time had come that He sent Jesus into the world. Israel's hope for the Messiah was centuries old, yet when He came, they did not understand or accept Him because they had taken their eyes off the one who had made the promise.

Faith and hope are the building blocks of love. Without hope we are reduced to our animal passions, existing only on instinct. God has given all mankind promises that are for whoever decides to walk in the hope of those promises. He has also given each of us promises that go beyond our human desires. He is a God of hope! By the power of His Spirit we can abound in hope with all joy and peace. This is my prayer for you. This is His promise to you.

Now the God of hope fill you with all joy and peace in believing, that ye may abound in hope, through the power of the Holy Ghost. (Romans 15:13)

Insights into Spiritual Portals: Portals of Hope

*For whatsoever things were written aforetime were
written for our learning, that we through patience
and comfort of the scriptures might have hope.*
(Romans 15:4)

In the passage above, the Apostle Paul tells us that the
episodes of life recorded in the Bible are examples to us
that through patience we may have the same realization
of fulfilled hope as those whose stories are contained in
the Scriptures. We can have hope in anything that God
has promised us, as long as our desire and patience en-
dure. This is where considering the stories of others who
have had their godly hopes realized can benefit us who
likewise have the hope of His promises.

The Book of Ruth tells the story of a non-Israelite
woman who in much adversity found a home, a husband, a son, a family, a God, and a destiny through hope.
Patience is a characteristic that always accompanies
hope. Patience does not mean that we sit idly by until
something happens but that, like Ruth, we vigorously

pursue our expected hope through persistent action and faithfulness. Being faithful in doing the things you know to do will always reap a great reward in your life. This open portal will always yield the godly hope that has been given to you.

Personal Application

Hope is a necessary component of spiritual life. Anyone who lives beyond the moment and plans for the future must have hope for the things they believe will happen but have not yet come to pass. Three key ingredients in acquiring godly hope are *patience*, *trust*, and *confirmation*. These three build in us the confidence of hope, and the faith built by this confidence is an assurance that what is being hoped for will come to pass.

Since hope relates to something that has not yet happened, *patience* is required to allow all things to work in the timing of God. If God is in my hope, I can wait patiently for its answer; otherwise, I am continually frustrated and agitated because my desire has not yet materialized.

Trust focuses us on our source of hope. We must

examine ourselves to see if the source of our hope is our human desire or God.

Confirmation validates the source of my hope. When I am confident that God and His will are the source of my hope, it gives me peace and rest. Impatience and frustration are signs that my hope may not be based in God.

> Impatience and frustration are signs that my hope may not be based in God.

What specific things are the sources of your hope?

Do you trust? Trust gives you a confidence that what you hope for will come to pass, regardless of current circumstances.

Is your hope based on what you desire as confirmed by God? Do you have the certainty that God's will is in the thing you are hoping for?

Amaze us, O God, by the power of hope!

CHAPTER EIGHT

Amazing Selflessness

*It is a spiritual axiom—the more of God the less of self
and the more of self the less of God. Selfless people are
perhaps the most admired people because they teach us
the virtue of sacrifice by their willingness to love.*

—ROGER ROTH

I saw her sitting on the front row patiently waiting her
turn to speak with me. On either side she had her
grandchildren—three of them—huddled close by.

Most of us were aware of the circumstances surrounding her personal sacrifice in refusing to allow
social services to place the children in foster homes. She
had insisted to the court that regardless of the parents'
inability, she was still their family and more than able
and willing to rear them. The court reluctantly agreed

and, knowing her meager income, many of the congregation shared clothes, toys, and occasional food boxes to assist in her brave effort.

I was sitting in my usual post-service place—an extended step area directly in front of the preaching podium. It was specifically designed for a chair to be placed so that I could, while seated, speak and minister face-to-face with those who came forward. This was my way of bridging the chasm between the pulpit and the pew.

While hundreds pressed their way toward the exits, chatting and saying good-bye to friends, those with specific interests or needs could move forward. I wanted to be accessible—they knew I would take "all comers."

Often the lights in the auditorium were dim and the hour late when I finally made my way to my study. I had by that time viewed children's school pictures, prayed for pets, litigated marital problems, interceded for lost loved ones, rebuked devils, and prayed for deliverance and healing for most every affliction known to mankind.

It was finally her turn, and this precious grandmother pushed her little brood toward me. While I busied myself greeting each of them, she said, "Brother Hanby, I need you to pray for my grandchildren."

I looked at their sparkling eyes and chubby cheeks—they looked fine to me. "What seems to be the problem?" I asked.

"I just want to be sure that they will be loved and cared for when I am gone," Willy Mae replied.

I looked at her and lightheartedly replied, "And where are you planning to go?"

She reached up and lifted a portion of her gray hair, which was combed in a swirl above her forehead. There I was shocked to see an ugly ulcer, larger than a silver dollar, sunken into her skull. She immediately went on to say, "I was at Peter Smith [the county hospital] this week, and the doctors say that the cancer is already into my brain. There is really nothing they can do." I started to speak, but she continued, "Now, Pastor, don't worry about me. I just want you to lay your hands on the children so that I can be sure they'll be okay."

Her request was like a command, and I began praying for each of the children. Then I reached out and

> "I just want to be sure that they will be loved and cared for when I am gone."

placed my hands on either side of her face and rebuked the cancer. As I made my way to the study, all I could think was that she didn't even ask me to pray for her terminal condition. Her selflessness was totally amazing.

The following Sunday service was in full swing—singing, worshipping, and clapping—when to my surprise, Willy Mae, normally shy and withdrawn, marched boldly down the center aisle with her grandchildren in tow. She beckoned to me, and as I leaned toward her, she took the microphone from my hand, turned, lifted the lock of her hair and announced that the cancer had fallen off into her lap on Monday morning while she was driving the grandchildren to school!

Most of the congregation had no clue that she'd had cancer. All they could see was a slick shiny spot on the top of her forehead. As I retrieved the microphone and explained what had happened the previous Sunday, the entire congregation exploded in powerful praise and faith. Miracles began happening spontaneously throughout the congregation.

I was informed recently that Willy Mae has passed away, some thirty years after that event. Like the woman in the Bible who broke the alabaster box, her story has been told all over the world, a memorial to her amazing selflessness.

Selflessness Touches God

Selflessness, as the word indicates, is being less concerned with yourself than with others. It is an antonym of selfishness. Selfish people are always trying to hold on to things or advance their position with other people. Selfless people work to advance good toward other people.

Selfishness is really a form of fear, whereas selflessness is an attribute of love. Selfless people like Florence Nightingale, Mother Teresa, William Wilberforce, and others are often admired because of the sacrifice they displayed in their willingness to obey God by serving others.

Selfless people do amazing things. Florence Nightingale helped reform medical and sanitation practices, saving thousands of people. Mother Teresa ministered to the orphans and outcasts in India. William Wilberforce worked tirelessly to end the slave trade. These and others are not remembered for their great fortunes or positions of power but for a love that put others before self. That is what selfless people do.

Acts of selflessness are usually difficult because they involve a personal cost. The cost of sacrifice is what makes them selfless acts—the greater the sacrifice the more significant the selfless act.

> Acts of selflessness involve a personal cost.

Insights into Spiritual Portals: A Selfless Nature

> Greater love hath no man than this, that a man lay down his life for his friends. (John 15:13)

Selflessness is a quality that is universally admired. The greatest act of selflessness is to, as Jesus said, lay down your life for your friends. We can view this as the actual act of physically dying in place of another, as in Charles Dickens' *The Tale of Two Cities*, where Sydney Carton takes the place of Charles Darnay on the guillotine. We all, however, have the ability to do this selfless deed on a daily basis without the finality of physical death, by dying to selfish emotions and desires in order to benefit others. This is the example that Willy Mae provided for us and the example that is seen in many Bible figures.

"[Jesus], when he was reviled, reviled not again; when he suffered, he threatened not; but committed himself to him that judgeth righteously" (1 Peter 2:23). This type of laying down your life (your personal desires and dreams) for the greater purpose of God to affect others through your obedience requires great selflessness. Moses was a ruler of Egypt but gave up his exalted position and his future for the purpose of leading Israel out of bondage. This decision opened many spiritual portals for Moses and for Israel.

Your willingness to overcome the unjust criticism of others, to find your peace in God rather than in the opinions of people, to do the hard and honorable thing instead of the easier and more materially rewarding option, opens for you unbelievable portals. For Willy Mae, it provided not only a miraculous healing but also the joy and accomplishment of using her life to benefit and perfect others. If your desire is greater than material blessing, if your greater desire is in spiritual reward and advancement, then your willingness to become a selfless minister of good will provide access to many spiritual portals.

Personal Application

When you ask God to teach you to be selfless, He will do it. We are not asked to save or help the whole world but only those God puts in our care. One of the steps in selfless acts is to determine to whom God is sending you.

"Of them which thou gavest me have I lost none" (John 18:9). Jesus saved the whole world, but He ministered personally to only a very small percentage of those alive in His day. It is important to know those whom God has given you, in order to know to whom you are to minister.

Willy Mae displayed unique selflessness by caring for her grandchildren, while Martin Luther King was involved with an entire nation and David Livingstone served a whole continent. None of their sacrifices were more significant than those of the others—only their fields were different.

If you want God to give to you amazing selflessness,

ask Him to show you your field, to show you those He has given you.

Then ask Him to remove from you all fear of loss and put you actively into the lives of those with need.

Amaze us, O God, by the power of selflessness!

CHAPTER NINE

Amazing Coincidence

God is a God of coincidence. He orchestrates two events and times them perfectly to intersect with your need and His purpose. Entering the coincidence portal starts by being awakened to the presence of God in every spiritual coincidence.

—MARK HANBY

The idea of coincidence is common to all individuals. We frequently allude to some event by saying, "What a coincidence!" But is what we call coincidence just mere chance or could it be a divine appointment?

Coincidence 1: On the way to the mall you are thinking about someone you haven't seen for a while. The last time you spoke, you left on very bad terms and have not wanted to see that person since. While walking the aisles of a store, you come face-to-face with the person about whom you had thought only minutes before. You exclaim, "What a coincidence! I was just thinking about you!" As a result you reconcile your differences and renew your friendship. Is this just chance or is it a divine appointment?

Coincidence 2: You are looking for a new job in your field of experience. Your wife asks you to go to a party at her friend's house—which you are reluctant to do, because you never seem to have a good time with that particular crowd. You finally yield to her repeated requests.

That night you speak with someone, and the topic of a job opening in your field comes up. You eventually get the job and later remark to your wife, "That was quite a coincidence. If you hadn't persisted in asking me to go to that party, I would have missed out on this job." Is this mere chance or divine appointment?

Coincidence 3: You work in a department store and think, "God, it would be great if I could afford to buy some clothes. It's been a long time since I've had any-thing new to wear." From out of the blue, corporate headquarters sends out a memo the next day instructing the manager to reward you with $500 in merchandise. You say, "This is a fantastic coincidence; only yesterday I was thinking how nice it would be if I could only af-ford some new clothes." Is this mere chance or divine appointment?

Coincidence 4: You've been looking for someone to settle down with, but it seems every date with a new person only ends in the frustrating thought, *Is there anyone out there for me?* On top of that, your current job is coming to an end. This causes you to consider your options, and you decide to join the military.

Of all the places they could send you for training, Baltimore is the place where the military has its school for your specialty. While there, you remember a girl you had met one time some years earlier and ask if she would like to meet. She remembers you and later tells you that it was good you called when you did, for she was thinking of a career change and would have shortly left the area.

Long story short, you fall in love and marry. You say, "Now that was quite a series of coincidences! If I had not been in need of a better job and had not decided to join the military and chosen that field of training and if the military had not sent me to Baltimore when they did, we would never have gotten together." Is this mere chance or divine appointment?

All four of these short examples happened to real people. We often think of a coincidence as a chance meeting or two or more things that are accidentally linked. In other words, we think of them as things that just happened without planning.

Divine Appointments

May I suggest that much of what we call coincidence is really a divine appointment in the forethought of God? What we could call a "God coincidence" is divinely orchestrated incidents

> Much of what we call coincidence is really a divine appointment in the forethought of God.

intersecting at an appointed time. In happening at the same time, they cause us to enter a divine appointment with something God has prepared for us.

Amazing acts of God can often be explained as God coincidences. When you say, *Amaze me, O God*, you are in effect asking God to take something in heaven that is finished and not subject to time and bring it into your earthly experience where things are incomplete and in time. The intersecting of this heavenly reality with your earthly need or desire is a divine appointment, or God coincidence.

The difference between having a coincidental happening and a divine appointment is in our perception of the events. To the person who gives no place to the miraculous, God's intervention is nothing more than a chance happening with either a good or unpleasant outcome, so the event, for them, ends. It provides for them no greater understanding, no discovery into the ongoing plan of God for their lives, no increased awe or appreciation for God or the miraculous.

To the person who recognizes the hand of God in events, even unpleasant events, every episode is filled with divine purpose. To that person, a coincidence can become a window to the operation of God and a stepping-stone to greater understanding and divine cooperation.

The realization that God is always active in our lives and an ever-present participant in our affairs lends purpose to our existence and provides for us an understanding and a security in the knowledge that we do not walk this life alone. We each have purpose, but more important, we each have a tremendous destiny. Purpose is a vehicle to help us arrive at our destiny, but destiny is the principal thing.

Divine coincidence, in one degree or another, happens to everyone, but the ability to see these occurrences as more than just mere chance allows us to become participants in God's plan rather than merely interested bystanders.

An Amazing Series of Coincidences

My grandson and I had been planning our three-day camping trip for a while. Mason is eight years old and extremely addicted to the outdoors. Somehow he

finds great meaning in rocks, sticks, and various spe-
cies of bugs, all of which he insists on bringing to me,
along with his dialogue concerning their purpose and
importance.

He is also very good at observing visible wildlife,
which he insists are "right over there." These elusive
creatures range from dinosaurs to polar bears, which, as
you know, are very rare in North Texas. On one of our
last trips, he even spotted a megalodon shark swimming
in the shallow stream below our camp and expressed
great disappointment that I, the consummate hunter,
had somehow failed to see it.

Our trip in the pickup took about three hours, and
Mason worked diligently on advancing SpongeBob to
another level on his Nintendo DS while I conducted
some unfinished business on my cell phone. We crossed
the Red River and drove through the Arbuckle Moun-
tains, eventually stopping at Walmart in Ada, Oklahoma, for our final food supplies.

I pushed my grocery cart along searching for those
nutritious items that I knew he would eat—hot dogs,
ketchup, white buns, marshmallows, ramen noodles,
Lucky Charms, Hershey Bars, lollipops, et cetera. Veg-

etables and whole wheat were definitely not on Mason's list. He had already pleaded for me to later stop by McDonald's so that he could stock up on chicken nuggets—a request I had denied. I was about to suggest grilled chicken legs, but he had disappeared. I knew I would eventually find him in the toy department.

I was on my way to collect him when he came hurrying toward me toting a rather large box of Legos. Before I could object, he gushed, "Papa, you won't believe this, but these are on sale, and I know that no other store in the whole United States carries this set."

As I pushed him back toward the toy department, he continued to insist that, although there wasn't a cloud in the sky, inclement weather was upon us and that he would be bored out of his mind just sitting watching it rain for three days with no Legos to assemble.

There was a cart sitting squarely in front of the Lego shelf, and its owner, a grandmotherly type of woman, was searching up and down the aisle. "I am sorry," she said as she pulled the cart out of our way, and then she asked, "Would you happen to know where the Lincoln Logs are located?"

"Yes," I jovially replied, "I have six unopened boxes of them cluttering a closet at my house."

She said, "You wouldn't be interested in selling them, would you? I don't think they carry them here anymore."

Without waiting for an answer, she leaned down toward Mason and said, "Sweetheart, you should be very grateful that you have folks who love and care for you. I have just received custody of my two grand-nephews. They are three and five years old and have been moved from home to home all of their lives. They have no clothes, shoes, or toys—I am having to round up everything."

She then looked back toward me and said, "They never learned to play constructively, and I thought the Lincoln Logs might be a good place to start."

I realized that we were in one of those God moments—an amazing coincidence where two pre-ordained things come together in one preordained moment—another way of saying a "God coincidence." Mason pushed his

> I realized that we were in one of those God moments—an amazing coincidence.

face against me and began weeping softly. She couldn't have known that just three years ago, my wife and I had adopted him after he had lived in twenty-one foster homes in less than one year.

She also could not have known that many years ago, a man (whom I had considered somewhat off-the-wall until now) had heard in one of my messages that some fifty years before as a child I had enjoyed playing with Lincoln Logs. In some weird tribute understood only to him, he had sent me six large boxes of them. To this day, I cannot explain why, while moving three different times and selling excess items ranging from antique organs to grandfather clocks, I had managed to keep the Lincoln Logs.

It had to have been an intervention by God to reserve these Logs for a much higher spiritual purpose. How many things in our life that we consider oddities or strange happenings are, unknown to us at the time, really the hand of God?

I quietly prayed for her and the children, then asked for her information, promising to stay in touch. This week Mason and I are planning another trip to Oklahoma. We are not camping this time. We've gathered several bags of children's clothes, shoes, and toys for Allen and Roy, and of course we have the Lincoln Logs. I called Mrs. West this morning and told her that we were coming. She was so excited!

Before we left the store, my grandson said, "Papa, I don't really need the Legos." He had been taken into a spiritual moment just as I had. In comparison to spiritual moments, supernatural things lose their luster.

You probably know that when we checked out of Walmart that day, there was a box of Legos in our cart that "couldn't have been found in any other store in the whole United States." And it was true that, although Legos can be found in most stores, only the desire for those Legos at that time was able to precipitate this divine appointment—and by the way, it didn't rain!

Divine Coincidence Is
Always a Sign of God

When I am in my sixties, a man from New York "just happens" to sends me six new boxes of Lincoln Logs—like I'm really inclined to play with them at my age. I move hundreds of miles and leave many valuable items behind but "just happen" to take the Logs. Years later, I "just happen" to be in a store and my grandson "just happens" to wander to the toy aisle at the same time a tender woman "just happens" to be looking for the item to help her grandnephews. As a result God has an opportunity to minister to her and her family and me and mine as well. Is this merely a coincidence or a divine appointment?

I suggest it is the latter. Signs of God in your life don't "just happen." They are a series of coincidences that by themselves are seemingly insignificant but put together become a marvelous sign of God. It is a divine appointment that reveals His nature and that nothing in our lives is insignificant—not even six boxes of Lincoln Logs given to an older man.

> God has been making preparations in your life for years that will find their divine appointment in your future.

How many things that have occurred in your life yesterday, last month, or years before are waiting to intersect with a preordained moment in your life? God has been making preparations in your life for years that will find their divine appointment in your future. If you are willing to ask, "Amaze me, O God," you will recognize them for what they are when they happen.

Insights into Spiritual Portals: Life's Coincidences

"It came to pass" is a phrase that is sometimes used in the Bible to introduce amazing coincidences. It often carries with it the thought that something destined to happen in the heavenly dimension has occurred in the earthly dimension. It is like having the doors on both sides of the platform opening simultaneously. This particular phrase occurs hundreds of times in scripture with powerful implications regarding God's spiritual timing. To know how God's timing operates in your life is a key to your peace and patience. When God's timing intersects with His purpose, what we think of as coincidences occur in our life.

In the book of Acts, chapter 9, we have several examples of this phrase ushering in God's purpose. As Peter traveled through Lydda, he found Aeneas, who was bedridden for eight years. Not only was Aeneas healed, but the whole of that area was spiritually changed. Then because Peter happened to be near the city of Joppa (coincidence?) when Tabitha died, he was summoned and God raised her from the dead. Finally, there was a group of Gentiles who were seeking God; and the Spirit—through miraculous events—used Peter to minister the Holy Spirit to them. Each of these instances is initiated by the phrase "and it came to pass." These were divine coincidences. The timing of God and the purpose of God intersected in each of these coincidental events.

In each of our lives, God operates in a similar fashion. There are things He has purposed for each of us. His timing and purpose intersect often in our lives in ways many of us do not recognize. Our life is not made up of chance happenings but has purpose and destiny. What seem to us as chance meetings with acquaintances or fortunate occurrences leading to employment or a physical healing or events ushering in lifelong relationships are not mere chance but divine coincidence. Understanding this and seeking to find God in all these events—even events that are uncomfortable and unpleasant—can help prepare and position us for the next time the doors on both sides of the platform open.

Personal Application

Distinguishing what we consider mere coincidence from God coincidence often lies in our perception of the event. Some coincidences only become recognized as God coincidences when they occur with other events. The receiving of the Lincoln Logs as a consequence of a statement I made in one of my messages may be considered a mere coincidence, but it became a God coincidence when it became part of the events that occurred that day in the Walmart in Ada, Oklahoma.

> Distinguishing what we consider mere coincidence from God coincidence often lies in our perception of the event.

Think about some events that could be described as coincidences you have had. In what ways could they be considered God coincidences?

If you don't see them as God coincidences yet, be

aware that God may use them in your future to do amazing things.

In the events that you would consider God coincidences, what do you think He was trying to say? What about His nature was revealed to you?

Amaze us, O God, by the power of coincidence!

CHAPTER TEN

Amazing Spiritual Awareness

The surest way to develop spiritual awareness is to consciously include God in everything you do by asking him to "Amaze me, O God."

The Bible tells us to draw close to God and He will draw close to us. The reason it tells us to draw close to God first is that He is always close to us. By consciously making an attempt to bring God into everything we do, we open a portal for the God who is always near to become active in our life.

—MARK HANBY

Every person in the history of mankind has experienced the direct influence of God in his or her life. God is continually speaking to us and acting on our behalf; however, we do not always comprehend it, and some people apparently never realize it.

One key to experiencing the amazement of God is to develop your spiritual awareness. There is perhaps no more powerful way to develop spiritual awareness than to trust God in difficult circumstances.

When you've come to the end of your abilities and to the end of your possibilities and are still in desperate need, fear often hinders your spiritual awareness. But this can also be the time of your greatest spiritual sensitivity if, in your need, you can look for signs of God.

Now I said signs *of* God and not signs *from* God—a distinction we discussed in chapter 1. We often seek a sign from God, but the spiritual person is not looking for a sign from God as much as a sign of God.

> The spiritual person is not looking for a sign from God as much as a sign of God.

A Sign of God

Some friends of mine have a gift of praying with people for physical healing and have been allowed by God to participate in more mighty miracles than they are able to remember. Eight years ago, a man who was dying of cancer came to them for prayer. For whatever reason, he loved ostriches. They were not only his favorite bird, they were the source of much wonder and study. He had pictures of ostriches on his wall, ceramic figurines placed around the house, and even ornaments of this stilted bird on his Christmas tree.

His wife, Sarah, had always believed in God, and she was severely shaken when her husband died a short time later. After all her prayers and the intercession of many believers, he still died, and her faith was understandably troubled.

These types of situations are at best very difficult, and meaningful explanations are illusive. Why does a good person who has given much to the world end up dying while an evil person who has preyed on people countless times and has shown no mercy for his victims seemingly escapes death at every turn?

To many, these inconsistencies do not seem right; and to Sarah, it didn't seem fair that she should lose such a good husband at a young age. As her pain and despair grew in the weeks following his death, Sarah began to doubt God. Her efforts to reconcile her concept of a good and faithful God with the suffering she was enduring led her to question God and His love for her.

The loss of her husband was difficult to accept but so was the feeling that God had somehow let her down.

> The loss of her husband was difficult to accept but so was the feeling that God had somehow let her down.

After all, she believed He had the power to deliver her husband and to spare her from this prolonged anguish; but for some reason He had not.

One winter's day she was washing dishes in her kitchen as another bout of grief passed over her. As she fell to the floor she cried, as no doubt we all have at some distressful time in our life, "God, are you real? I just need to know you're here and you care!"

As she opened her tear-filled eyes, she saw a sign of God. Looking out her kitchen window, she saw an ostrich feather floating gently by. She ran out in the snow to retrieve it. As Sarah held it in her hand, she understood it as not only a sign from God but more important a sign of God—a sign of His faithfulness and love, a sign of His continual nearness to her. Other friends and family members witnessed similar things.

An ostrich feather in the middle of winter comes floating down on a continent where ostriches do not live, in front of a window where at that exact moment a mournful woman in confusion is seeking confirmation of God and His goodness. Some might say it's "merely a coincidence." To those, however, who know the operation of God and are seeking His continual reality, it is an answer to the heart that summons Him to "Amaze us, O God!"

Jacob Provides a Pattern for Us

And Jacob went out from Beersheba, and went toward Haran. And he lighted upon a certain place, and tarried there all night, because the sun was set; and he took of the stones of that place, and put them for his pillows, and lay down in that place to sleep. And he dreamed, and behold a ladder set up on the earth, and the top of it reached to heaven: and behold the angels of God ascending and descending on it. And, behold, the Lord stood above it, and said, I am the LORD God of Abraham thy father, and the God of Isaac: the land whereon thou liest, to thee will I give it, and to thy seed; And thy seed shall be as the dust of the earth, and thou shalt spread abroad to the west, and to the east, and to the north, and to the south: and in thee and in thy seed shall all the families of the earth be blessed. And, behold, I am with thee, and will keep thee in all places whither thou goest, and will bring thee again into this land; for I will not leave thee, until I have done that which I have spoken to thee of. And Jacob awaked out of his sleep, and he said, Surely the

LORD *is in this place; and I knew it not.* (Genesis 28:10–16)

Jacob was traveling in unfamiliar territory. He was sent on a journey by his father to find a wife. His thought was to find her and bring her back, but little did he know the journey would take him over twenty years and be fraught with many twists and turns leading to unforeseen events, deceptions, dangers, and coincidences. He did not see the bigger picture, but coincidence and divine confirmation did let him know that God was with him.

In our life we do not always see the bigger picture, but if we have confirmation that God is with us, we can have confidence in all we do. Jacob certainly did not intend to stay away two decades. What a strange coincidence that as he is on a journey out of the land, God gives him a confirmation in a dream that he will be returning and possess the land and have a multitude of descendants that will bless the entire earth.

> If we have confirmation that God is with us, we can have confidence in all we do.

He did not respond by saying, "What a strange dream," but by acknowledging that it was God, and the coincidence of the dream coupled with his departure from his homeland gave him illumination—"Surely the LORD is in this place; and I knew it not."

This story is an allegory for us as well. On the journey of life, God is always with us, even if we don't realize it at the time. As confirmations of His love and purpose, God gave Sarah an ostrich feather, He gave Jacob a dream, and He gives each of us numerous instances that intersect at His appointed time to confirm His love, to provide comfort, and to direct us toward our destiny.

Insights into Spiritual Portals: Spiritual Awareness

> *And he said, Who art thou, Lord? And the Lord said, I am Jesus whom thou persecutest: it is hard for thee to kick against the pricks. And he trembling and astonished said, Lord, what wilt thou have me to do?* (Acts 9:5–6)

The Apostle Paul was perhaps the greatest persecutor of the early church—beating, imprisoning, and killing many of that early faith. Yet even during his malicious activities, God was active in his life. Religious training has conditioned many of us to believe that God is only active in our lives when we think and act properly. But God is continually involved in our lives in very active ways. How He is able to act may be conditioned upon our attitude and actions, but He is always involved in our life in numerous ways. We may not always have been interested in God, but He has always been interested in us. There was a day when a great portal opened for the Apostle Paul. He was struck down, and Jesus spoke to him with words of conviction. Paul's initial response was to ask, "Who art thou, Lord?" In stressful circumstances we often ask similar things. "God, are you there? What am I supposed to do? What does this all mean?" These are questions that can open portals for us if we recognize and have confidence that God is on the other side of our question waiting to respond.

Personal Application

It is generally easier for us to see the hand of God in things we consider to be blessings, rather than in difficult, stressful events or those that cause us personal or financial loss. Yet demanding situations can be cause for witnessing the amazing power of God. We all probably ask God to bless us, but not many of us, I would think, say to God, "Discipline me," or "Teach me submission to your authority!"

One reason we are not always aware of God is that we have been conditioned to see Him only as part of pleasant experiences or experiences that we perceive as having worked out for good. It is becoming aware of God in our struggles that most deepens our awareness of God and the way He acts.

We have been conditioned to see God only as part of pleasant experiences.

Unfortunately many ascribe to the enemy acts that actually come from God. The Bible tells us of a God who sometimes acts contrary to our perception of Him. God cursed the ground for the benefit of mankind (Genesis 3:17). It pleased God to make Jesus a sacrifice for sins (Isaiah 53:10). We, as did Jesus, learn obedience through the things we suffer (Hebrews 5:8). And our afflictions can work toward our benefit (2 Corinthians 4:17).

Awareness of God becomes most heightened when we see His hand in our suffering as well as in what we consider blessings.

Think of a time when God felt especially far away. It was probably at some low point in your life. Can you see how God was in the events? In hindsight, was the episode, though painful, beneficial to your spiritual maturity?

Think of some past occurrence when your own actions or those of someone else caused you pain or distress. How was God revealed to you through that situation?

Now think of some pain that you may have inflicted upon someone else in your immaturity that you now regret. What did this teach you about God?

God is always in our life, whether we are aware of Him or not.

Amaze us, O God, by the power of awareness!

CHAPTER ELEVEN

Amazing Compassion

I have found the paradox, that if you love until it hurts, there can be no more hurt, only more love.

—MOTHER TERESA

Sympathy prompts our concern but empathy activates our compassion.

—ROGER ROTH

When I topped the hill, I could see the flashing lights and people moving from their cars to the center median of the thoroughfare. My first thought was to turn onto a side street and bypass the accident. Traffic was backing up, and I needed to make a quick decision.

Having spent most of the day in my study preparing for the evening midweek Bible study, I was anxious to get home, dressed, and back to minister to our thriving young congregation. As I slowed to turn, I heard a voice in my spirit directing me to stop. I knew immediately that I had to be here—I had to see what had happened.

I stepped out of my car and moved closer to the scene—then I heard him—an almost insane childish scream, over and over again—"I want my daddy!"

An unusual authority came over me and I boldly said to the police officer who was urging everyone to stay back, "I am a man of God." I was as shocked as he by the words that came out of my mouth. Rather than protesting, he took me by the arm and pulled me toward the grotesque crumpled heap lying in the grass.

The boy was eight years old and the twisted frame of the bicycle lying on his small body mutely explained the crisis. He screamed again . . . "I want my daddy!" . . . and I focused on his bloody face.

One of the handlebars was embedded in his forehead just below the hairline. I was shocked that the child could possibly be conscious and concerned that he probably would not live long enough to receive medical attention. I dropped to my knees beside him and as he struggled to focus through the blood and gore, he cried, "Are you my daddy?"

Something happened in that moment that changed my life forever. Right before my eyes his face morphed into the face of my oldest son and then into the face of my second son and I answered, "Yes, I am your daddy." A visible peace came over the boy as I began to pray in the spirit, not with concern for some father's son but rather with heartrending compassion fueled by an overwhelming personal love.

Oblivious to the crowd pressing in, I continued to rebuke death and command life until the police officer gently pulled me back, saying that the ambulance had arrived.

Oblivious to the crowd pressing in, I continued to rebuke death and command life.

Later that evening, I sat with Timmy's parents in the chapel of All Saints Hospital. We wept together and thanked God as the surgeon announced that Timmy was going to make a complete recovery!

I am not sure which was more amazing—the miracle of a child's recovery or the miracle of compassion that forever changed the ministry of a young pastor.

The Distinction Between Concern and Compassion

There is a difference between possessing compassion versus having concern, and a distinction between being moved by empathy versus being motivated by sympathy. Sympathy will generate concern, but empathy has the ability to produce compassion.

Most of the people gathered that day around the sight of this unfortunate boy were sympathetic. They showed their concern in a number of ways, but concern is not the key to bringing forth God's amazing power; compassion is, and it invites a heavenly response.

Where concern can motivate us to pray, compassion will prompt us to act. Where concern may move us to give of our possessions, compassion awakens us to give of ourselves. Where sympathy leads us to show concern and respect, empathy spurs compassion by arousing us to invest ourselves in others.

Concern is a result of our mind, but compassion comes from what the Bible calls "our innermost being." Concern is an element of the soul, but compassion is an attribute of the spirit.

The word *concern* comes from the Latin word *concernere,* meaning with sifting or with the ability to prioritize and assign more significance to some things than to others. It involves a mental judgment related to the sifting of facts or evidence. Compassion comes from the Latin stem *compati,* meaning to suffer with. So where concern engages our minds, compassion engages our emotions and spirits by our willingness to suffer with or to be part of the process to help another.

> Where concern engages our minds, compassion engages our emotions and spirits.

When we have empathy, we in essence are so connected to the person or situation that we can see ourselves as them in the situation. Compassion causes

God's virtue to flow through us to the person or event on which we are focusing.

Compassion Triggers
Amazing Things

And there came a leper to him, beseeching him, and kneeling down to him, and saying unto him, If thou wilt, thou canst make me clean. And Jesus, moved with compassion, put forth his hand, and touched him, and saith unto him, I will; be thou clean. And as soon as he had spoken, immediately the leprosy departed from him, and he was cleansed. (Mark 1:40–42)

Genuine concern requires a measure of love, but compassion is evidence of a progressive love. All the attributes of God come to us in measure. So the Bible speaks to us about having peace and having perfect peace, about having grace and having great grace, about having joy and having full joy, and about having love and having perfect love.

We cannot make ourselves compassionate simply by

willing it, but we can learn to progress from concern toward compassion. It is natural that the people closest to you and the situations with which you are most familiar exude greater compassion. It is easier to be moved by that which may cause you the greatest loss or those with whom you have the deepest relationship.

Jesus had this inimitable ability to have compassion even on those he only just met. The incident of the leper, cited above, was not unique to His ministry. Jesus "went about doing good, and healing all that were oppressed of the devil" (Acts 10:38), in large degree as a direct consequence of His enormous compassion.

When Jesus saw this man whose body had become a mass of rotting flesh, he was "moved with compassion." To Jesus, this was not just someone with a great need but someone whose faith and infirmity touched Jesus' heart. Jesus not only understood what the leper was going through but by compassion experienced the man's condition as if it were His own.

His compassion gave him the ability to comprehend the fear, pain, and hopelessness of this man's condition. The leper's faith—*if thou wilt, thou canst make me clean*—gave Jesus permission to act on his behalf, but it was Jesus' compassion that empowered and caused him to act—*I will; be thou clean.*

Insights into Spiritual Portals: The Portal of Compassion

> *But a certain Samaritan, as he journeyed, came where*
> *he was: and when he saw him, he had compassion on*
> *him, And went to him, and bound up his wounds,*
> *pouring in oil and wine, and set him on his own beast,*
> *and brought him to an inn, and took care of him.*
> (Luke 10:33–34)

Compassion requires openness to the plight of others; it requires a determination not to fear, and it requires a freedom from the opinion of others. Your proper response to those around you opens you to the spiritual world. The good Samaritan had reason to fear for his life in helping the injured man. The same thieves may have been lying in wait for him as well. He did not know this unfortunate individual, and there was no natural reward that he could expect for helping this wounded and penniless individual. The priest and Levite saw no personal benefit in extending care to him. What made the Samaritan do it? Compassion. He had a desire to do good without any consideration of return. The priest and Levite lacked compassion, yet the Samaritan had it.

Compassion usually comes to people who have suffered successfully and to people who are able to put themselves in the place of another. The next time you are confronted by a human situation that demands a response, make an effort to put yourself in the place of the individual in need. This will mollify your fears and allow you to respond properly and in so doing unlock the miraculous.

> Compassion usually comes to people who have suffered successfully.

Personal Application

If we cannot will ourselves to have compassion, then how do we acquire it? Compassion is the ability to see a situation from God's perspective and to respond for the good of another. Compassion therefore requires us to put ourselves in the place of the other person and to be an instrument of God's love through which the power of God can flow.

When the love of God is manifested, we call it virtue. When the woman with the issue of blood received her healing by secretly touching Jesus' garment, Jesus said, "Somebody hath touched me: for I perceive that virtue is gone out of me" (Luke 8:46). Virtue was His compassionate love flowing to the need of the woman.

Likewise, our compassion allows for the love of God to flow through us to another. Putting people above things is one way to stimulate compassion. As we give sacrificially of ourselves, a greater measure for having compassion comes back to us.

Compassion is the fruit of learning to "love thy neighbor as thyself" (Mark 12:31). Compassion is also a consequence of having a life in proper order: God first, others second, ourselves third, and material things last.

Amaze us, O God, by the power of compassion!

CHAPTER TWELVE

Amazing Prayer

The desire to pray is itself a prayer. The essence of prayer is not speaking to God but learning to look at God. In prayer God listens to our heart more than our words; our words only help us form the true thoughts and intents of our heart.

—ROGER ROTH

Simplicity is an attribute of spirituality. I have not encountered people who were preoccupied with possessions or overly focused on natural activities who also possessed simple faith and the blessings that are derived from it.

Children are not weighted down with the many concerns we adults carry. When we teach children to pray and to believe that God answers prayer, they tend to put it into practice. They don't create prequalifications about whether they should pray or if it makes sense; they just go and do it. The following story illustrates what I am saying.

A friend of mine had four children. They lived on several acres of land outside of town, so they were able to have a variety of pets. Their youngest daughter had asked for a pet, and of all things wanted some little chickens.

The parents purchased the chicks, and everything was good in their daughter's little corner of the world until one very cold winter day she awoke to find that the chicks had escaped their coop and had frozen in the cold.

The inclination of the parents was obviously to dispose of the dead chicks, but the little girl said, "Why don't we pray and put them in the oven?" Does God really give words of knowledge to little children? I believe He does. The parents thought it was a foolish exercise but did as requested to appease their daughter's insistence. To their great surprise, within a few minutes chirping came from the oven. The chicks were restored.

Now to many, this may seem rather silly, but not to this little girl. She prayed and she got her answer. To her,

God was as concerned with her "small" dilemma as He was with a major world crisis. God is limited only by the limitations we place on Him.

Your Prayers Are Already Answered in Heaven

I want to speak with you about a single aspect of prayer that demonstrates the power of God to do amazing things. It may give you an insight into prayer that you have not considered.

Everything in the heavenly dimension is perfect, complete, and in order. When God answers prayer, He does not change heaven but alters the earth. When we pray, we are not telling God anything He does not already know: "For your Father knoweth what things ye have need of, before ye ask him" (Matthew 6:8).

> When God answers prayer, He does not change heaven but alters the earth.

God is not surprised by our successes or failures, our

sins or our righteous deeds. No good thing we can do can make Him love us more, and no mistake can cause Him to love us less. He does not change His plan or His will in response to our actions, whether good or bad. How we align with His will and plan, however, does in part determine whether the things He has completed and purposed for us in heaven will come to pass in our earthly lifetime.

Everything God ever intended for you, every blessing and every answer to prayer, is already completed in the heavenly dimension. Prayer does not convince God to do anything He has not already purposed to do in His will.

A Prayer, an Answer, and an Acceptance

All answered prayer involves at least three things—a request, an answer, and our acceptance of the answer. When His answer and our will are the same, it is easy; the difficulty is when what He answers is different than what we want or expect.

Father, if thou be willing, remove this cup from me: nevertheless not my will, but thine, be done. (Luke 22:42)

In this one sentence Jesus spoke a prayer, received an answer, and accepted the answer. His desire was not to take on the cup of sin. I don't believe the cup was so much about His having to go to the cross as it was about taking on the sins of the world. He never knew sin and its debilitating effects to produce fear and separation.

I believe this was the cup he was looking to avoid. He prayed the prayer, and in the next clause He received and accepted the answer. It was not God's will to let the cup pass from Him, so Jesus said, "I'll do your will." Jesus' will became one with God's will.

Prayer really comes down to discovering the will of God and then adjusting our will to do His. Prayer allows our will to become one with His will. This is a great key to witnessing the amazing power of God.

In prayer we sometimes throw ourselves before God, asking Him to answer us according to our will and not His will. When we ask according to our will, we make it difficult for God to answer one prayer without rejecting another.

When we ask in our will for great riches and contentment, how does He answer if those riches would also bring with them great sorrow? If we ask for peace and great fame, how does He answer if having great fame would destroy our peace?

Seeing into the Heavens

I was preaching at a church one Sunday, and after service I saw a commotion on the right side of the platform and went over to investigate. An usher had fallen over, apparently from a heart attack, and was lying motionless upon the carpet. I sent one of the onlookers to summon an ambulance.

The usher was not breathing and began to take on the color of death. Everyone was concerned, and prayer in various ways was being offered for him. He lay there without moving or breathing for at least a half an hour. It was apparent that he had died, and everyone was wondering what was keeping the paramedics. I remember distinctly hearing in my spirit the words, "This is not his time. I still have work for him to do."

With that, I put forth my hand and said, "I rebuke death off of you: be restored." When I made that proclamation life reentered his body, and he was restored to health.

Those around had made the request for God to intervene. We understood His heavenly will when He spoke into my spirit, and then we proclaimed His will and it came to pass. The key to amazing prayer is being able to see into heaven in order to understand His will.

When our desire in prayer aligns with His will, then all that is necessary is our exercise of faith to bring that will to pass. When our desire and His will do not align, it becomes more challenging. The challenge is to discover, accept, and do the will of God.

I was summoned to the hospital to pray for an infant child. He was so frail and weak that it made my heart go out to the parents and to this little baby. God showed a vision that this boy would not live. This is not the answer I wanted. This did not seem fair, yet it was His will.

Now a great adjustment had to be made between our will and God's because they were obviously different.

What good does it do to pray our will when He clearly shows us His heavenly will that is different from ours? Knowing and accepting this changed not only our prayer but provided an acceptance and understanding, and allowed the comfort of God to be released in that situation.

Without going into the details of why this was not God's will when everything within us wanted it to be His will, these two stories do exemplify that seeing into the heavenly dimension is the key factor in all answered prayer. Even when we pray without understanding and we receive our desired answer, it is because what we were praying for happened to be in alignment with His will.

> Seeing into the heavenly dimension is the key factor in all answered prayer.

Doing the will of God is a spiritual exercise in seeing into the heavens. "Thy kingdom come. Thy will be done, as in heaven, so in earth" (Luke 11:2).

Prayer goes beyond that which you can do or receive to that which you can become. We often pray so God can hear our desire; we seldom pray to hear His desire. We ask for the laws of the universe to be annulled on our behalf so our will can be done rather than positioning ourselves according to His will.

This is why much of prayer sometimes comes down to trying to twist God's arm or somehow convince Him of all the reasons He should do the things we ask. We try to make deals with God: "If you do this for me God, I'll never do that again or I'll do whatever you ask of me." It makes prayer into an exercise of negotiation rather than one of discovery.

Since everything God has done or will do is already completed in the heavenly dimension ("for ever, O LORD, thy word is settled in heaven" [Psalms 119:89]), then prayer should become an avenue where what He has completed in the heavens can become a reality in our earthly dimension.

If when we pray we are looking to understand the will of God, to know what He knows, and to see what He sees, then we pray His answer rather than our desire. This is what Jesus meant when He said, "I say unto you, The Son can do nothing of himself, but what he seeth the Father do: for what things soever he doeth, these also doeth the Son likewise" (John 5:19).

Jesus was able to see the finished work of God in the

heavenly dimension and, therefore, He was able to bring it to pass in the earth. We, likewise, can do the same. We can learn to see and pray the answer.

The Three Dimensions of Prayer

Prayer has dimensions: "Ask, and it shall be given you; seek, and ye shall find; knock, and it shall be opened unto you: For every one that asketh receiveth; and he that seeketh findeth; and to him that knocketh it shall be opened" (Matthew 7:7–8).

We often wonder why we receive some things we ask for, while the answer to other prayers seems illusive.

Prayer must lead to understanding and submission of our demands to His will; prayer without understanding and submission is often superstition and wishful thinking. We receive some things simply by asking. If we don't receive an answer by simply asking, then we enter into the second dimension of prayer, which is to seek or search. This involves such things as searching the scriptures for insight or confirmation. The highest dimension in prayer is knocking.

Knocking is the process of seeing into the heavens and discovering the will of God. The following example may seek to illustrate the dimensions of prayer.

I was asked to pray for someone for a new job. He had urgent need of finding a better position. He said, "I've asked God for many months, and I can't seem to get an answer. When I apply for different positions for which I'm qualified, I always get a rejection."

I've known many people who have asked God for a new job and in short order received what they were looking for, but not everyone. Since God is not a respecter of persons, then He does not arbitrarily decide to answer one by saying yes and another by saying no; but the way He answers is in some way linked to His will.

This is the first dimension of prayer: ask and you shall receive. For this person, however, all he received was his need to continue to seek God.

I asked him, "Since you have not found a job simply by asking, what else have you prayed?" He looked at me with a stare. It was a question he had never pondered. I said, "Have you searched your heart or the Scripture or other people to see if there is anything else you should do or change or something you need to understand?"

Seek and you will find. I've witnessed this work for many people.

He came back three or four weeks later and told me that in thinking about what type of employee he was and after hearing responses from others, he came to understand that maybe he was not as good an employee as he had thought. Primarily, he said, "I have not been thankful for the job I've had, but I've been grumbly and irritable." When he realized this, it changed his work environment much for the better, but he still had not received any offers.

Knock and it shall be opened unto you. I then asked him what the will of God was for him in this situation. He frankly said, "I don't know, but God must want me to be able to provide for my family." The highest dimension of prayer is the third dimension. It is finding the will of God.

He came back several months later and told me the following story. "When I spoke with you after church the last time, I went home and seriously asked what I only superficially had spoken before. I said, 'Okay, God, what is it You want me to do? What job do You have for me? What is Your will?'

"I did this for a number of days, and many times thought, *What's the use? I'm not getting anything.* Then I had a dream that I went down into my basement and the water and drainpipes were leaking at every joint. I felt totally lost and inadequate, so I picked up a wrench, and when I waved it, all the leaks stopped. It was a strange dream, but I remembered it very clearly when I woke, and I thought, *I wonder what it would be like to be a plumber?*

"About a week later, someone came into the appliance store where I was working. We spoke awhile, and he handed me a card telling me that if I was ever interested in becoming a plumber to let him know. I would never have considered doing that kind of job except for the dream and my desire to know God's will. Now I have a different job from anything I would have imagined. I love the job, and it provides the income I need to provide for my family. I learned to knock, and He opened this job for me."

Insights into Spiritual Portals: Righteousness

Confess your faults one to another, and pray one for another, that ye may be healed. The effectual fervent prayer of a righteous man availeth much. Elias was a man subject to like passions as we are, and he prayed earnestly that it might not rain: and it rained not on the earth by the space of three years and six months. And he prayed again, and the heaven gave rain, and the earth brought forth her fruit. (James 5:16–18)

Elijah was a person just like us. He was not any more or less special, except that he had learned what perhaps some of us are still in the process of learning—to order his life in righteousness. There is great power in righteousness. God's righteousness, or "rightnesses," are His ways of being and doing. When we live and act according to God's nature, then we can be said to be righteous. This is why the Apostle James instructs us to confess our faults and to pray for one another. This brings us into alignment with God and with our fellow man. There is great power in right living. Elijah's righteousness in God's purpose allowed him to pray a prayer that caused it not to rain for three and a half years and then to pray another prayer and cause a downpour. His power in you and through you is determined by His plan and purpose for you and your willingness to align yourself with His will.

Personal Application

Learn to find and pray the will of God. There are several things that may help you in this. Try the following:

- Be open to the way God speaks—visions, dreams, through other people, in your thoughts, by circumstances, in the Scripture, etc.
- Use your prayer request to make your prayer about Him and not only about your need or desire.
- Become willing to change. All prayer should change us in some way. Look at yourself honestly by seeing yourself as God sees you.

Amaze us, O God, by the power of prayer!

Concluding
Thoughts

Study hall at Berne-Knox High School in upstate New York was typical, at least as far as I know. Very little academia was pursued; however, I became well-studied in various ways of communicating with my classmates without actually using words.

Notes were stealthily passed and hand signals recognized, while eye contact and facial expressions all became a polished means of addressing various subjects, few of which were required for graduation.

Being reared in the home of old-fashioned godly parents with a decided penchant for strict living, I was not permitted to participate in dances, proms, parties, or dating. I was further encouraged to shun the evil of sneaky activities and admonished to use study hall as a time to pray—to silently lift my thoughts toward God—which, by the way, I often did.

Being a rather bright student and very quickly picking up on the unspoken language of the high school underworld, I had come to recognize the subtle insinuations and suggestions of my fellow students, many of whom were not fellows at all.

Here, beyond the righteous eye of my parents, in this cesspool of youthful wonder, I chanced letting go the wild steeds of thought and mysterious possibilities of boy/girl relationships. In the back of my mind, I could hear my mother singing, "There's an all-seeing eye watching you," and at times, I heard what I thought to be the almost audible voice of my father preaching, "God knows your very thoughts" and "The very thought of evil is sin."

The "all-seeing eye" didn't bother me so much because I wasn't really doing anything, but the "evil thought" thing sent me spiraling in condemnation downward toward the place where, as written in one of my father's most-quoted scriptures (Mark 9:44), "the worm dieth not and the fire is not quenched."

This was one reason I started spending a lot of time

praying in study hall. I didn't make much spiritual progress, however, because about the time I had thoroughly repented and had once again been "washed in the blood," one of the "fellow" students would walk by, purposefully brushing my arm, and I could once again smell the smoke and burning flesh—lost, only fifteen seconds after being completely redeemed!

Many years later, my perception of God would be completely changed. I would come to know Him as the loving Lord, exchanging the "law of sin and death" with the "law of life in Christ Jesus" (Romans 8:2) that makes me free from the law of sin and death. In Him, there is no condemnation. Such love and grace is truly amazing.

Overcoming Misconceptions

I included this story because I think, in a humorous way, it illustrates many of the misconceptions we have about God. We sometimes look at God as being somehow removed from our daily lives. We take things that are normal—such as a youthful interest in the opposite sex—and out of fear of what could happen, make God's response into something we should fear.

I had great parents, a wonderful upbringing, and a spiritual heritage for which I am very thankful. There was a tendency, however, and I believe still is among many who hold closely to religion, to be more focused on sin than on God. There is definitely a biblical standard of conduct that we should follow, but to make God into an angry judge waiting to pounce upon our weakness brings Him down to our level rather than allowing us to rise to His lofty heights.

God Is an Amazing God

God is an amazing God not primarily for what He does but for who He is. This book has been filled with stories of the amazing healings, miracles, and interventions of God and also some of the amazing things that happened when God did not choose the miraculous route but nevertheless acted miraculously.

When we pray, "Amaze us, O God," the greatest thing He can do in response is to share with us His divine nature. Our expectation in God amazing us should always be focused on a continued and growing relationship with Him.

The Amazing Question

During the height of the great Fort Worth revival, we were blessed to contribute to the support of more than a hundred missionary families around the world. Large mahogany plaques fashioned in the shape of the various countries in which they served were mounted prominently around the prayer-room walls. Pictures of the families were placed around the countries as a constant reminder of their sacrifice and our determination to support them through prayer as well as finance.

In those days, my frequent ministry journeys were aimed at visiting and encouraging many of these brave warriors of the cross; and through the years, I eventually visited and ministered in more than sixty countries on six continents. As you may imagine, the events and circumstances that I encountered are too numerous to tell, and they often run together in my thoughts like an endless dream beyond proper time and sequence. There are, however, some pictures seared into my memory as clearly as if they had happened just yesterday.

One such event took place some thirty-five years ago in the impoverished country of Indonesia. My plane touched down in Djakarta more than twenty hours after leaving the Dallas Love Field International Airport. I was warmly greeted by the aging missionary couple who had been serving there for more than twenty-five years.

With my luggage loaded into their battered old van, we set off for the "compound," which I later learned was made up of their home and ministry buildings. It was surrounded by great walls topped with broken shards of glass and strung with razor wire to discourage thieves and beggars. "There you will be able to eat and rest," they explained. "The services begin tomorrow."

The ride from the airport to the compound was astonishing. I had never seen such a mass of humanity. The endless cacophony of sounds included shouting voices, pleading beggars, braying donkeys, and grunting oxen—all punctuated by the never-ceasing honking of horns as cars pushed paths through the human thoroughfares. These assailing sounds were mixed with the pungent odors of abject poverty—cooking fires, burning garbage, rancid meat, manure, and death.

Pastor White was engaged in an endless commentary, shouting above the surrounding noises in order to be heard. "This is called the city that never sleeps," he announced. "They actually sleep, but only half of them in the day and the other half of them at night, so that what you see here never stops." He went on to explain that to truly understand the population-to-land ratio in that part of Indonesia, you would have to move every human in North America into an area the size of the state of Delaware! He went on to say that each morning the "death wagons" collected those who had perished overnight and took the bodies outside the city to be burned.

I didn't sleep much. The noise outside the compound walls seemed everlasting. I also managed to lose thirteen pounds in ten days. I found it rather difficult to get past the little black things in the rice, which Mrs. White explained were the unavoidable flies—"They are well cooked, however, and certainly won't hurt you." This fancy fare, topped with a rather generous lump of buffalo butter, which smelled to me like fresh goat droppings, assisted in my weight loss.

The services were uneventful. I spent most of my efforts encouraging the missionaries and the couple of hundred people they had reached throughout the years.

Before leaving, I insisted that I wanted to take a walk outside the compound. The Whites reluctantly agreed to accompany me, encouraging me to leave my watch and any other valuables behind. We had pressed our way a few yards from the compound gate when we came upon an old withered woman chopping a maggot-ridden piece of buffalo meat to sell.

I instructed Mrs. White to ask her if she knew Jesus. The woman answered with a couple of sentences, and when I asked what her reply had been, Mrs. White tearfully replied, "She said, 'I have never heard of him; I am sure he doesn't live on this block.'"

I returned home to bountiful America, this great Christian nation, with thousands of beautiful church structures whose steeples point toward a God who rarely visits their auditoriums. Here, everyone has heard of Jesus—the amazing question is whether or not He actually lives on our block!

Acquiring an Amazing Expectation

As I pray, "Amaze me, O God," I am asking for various things, but nothing more significant than that the people of God be awakened to their destiny and that He once again visits us in the full power of His being. What we call the Christian church cannot keep pace with the world's birthrate, much less connect the world to an amazing God. If His love were ever allowed to be fully unleashed through His people, He would forever save the world not only from material poverty but, far more important, from a poverty of the spirit.

Through the years, I have come to personally understand that His ways are "past finding out" (Romans 11:33). About the time I think I have the keys to God's miraculous manifestation, He amazes me again by doing something far beyond the realm of my expectation.

We have found Him, but we have not found Him out! As the old hymn says and the Bible illustrates, God truly does "move in mysterious ways, His wonders to perform."

So while we can never know all the ways of God,

there are some things we can be sure of. God is good, His truth is everlasting, His mercy endures to all generations, God cannot lie, His very essence is love, He has all power, and He can do anything. This magnificent God is moved with compassion, pleased with faith, obligated by His word, worthy of trust, acts sovereignly through order, and manifests Himself in glory.

This precious Lord will not withhold any good thing from them who ask Him (see John 14:14 and Matthew 18:19).

In the final analysis, God is simply not like us. He does not love like us, respond like us, or care like us. God is not governed by lack or need and also does not respond to human effort. He operates in a much higher order supplying our needs "according to His riches in glory" (Philippians 4:19).

Glory is the only atmosphere in which God manifests power—no glory, no manifestation. It should, therefore, become our life's pursuit to create this glorious atmosphere in which He is enthroned, a platform on which He may perform, a stage on which He may act! Then according to His infinite knowledge, absolute righteousness, and eternally finished work, He may manifest His will and purpose in our lives, amazing us with His goodness.

So then, rather than trying through prayer and works to twist God to our agenda, we enter into His finished work, which He has willed for us before the foundation of the world. Some would argue, "Then why pray?" We do not pray to convince God! He already knows our need. We pray to open the earthly portals so that the heavenly answers may pass through. The Spirit "searcheth all things, yea, the deep things of God" (1 Corinthians 2:10) so that we may speak in the earth the will of God. "Thy kingdom come, Thy will be done in earth, as it is in heaven" (Matthew 6:10).

When we hear a word from God in our spirit or when we receive a promise from God through His Word, we should begin creating our atmosphere, our platform, our stage, because God will always come back by way of His promise. If He said it, He will perform it!

Romans, chapter 8, verses 19 through 23, tell us that the whole earth is groaning and that we also are groaning within ourselves. Verse 19 states that we are waiting for a "manifestation of the sons of God." This does not mean that men are manifested but rather that the "whole creation" is waiting for God's children to prepare and provide an atmosphere in which God may manifest His eternal purposes. The same scripture calls this an "earnest expectation."

I have often been asked why I have been blessed to witness so many unusual and miraculous things through the years and my answer is always the same: It is certainly not because I have been better or more spiritual than others. I have simply had the courage to refuse the chains of religious bondage and live in holy expectation of God's amazing intervention.

Expect God to amaze you!

A FINAL WORD OF ENCOURAGEMENT

The entire process of life, in reality, is very straightforward and comes down to this one simple truth: "For it is God which worketh in you both to will and to do of his good pleasure" (Philippians 2:13). God is working in you, in various ways, so that you desire and do the will of God.

When God reestablishes the fullness of His Kingdom on earth, it will not be because He beat the living daylights out of anyone who was in opposition to His rule and forced them to follow His ways. It will not come through force, using His power to make the world follow Him, but through a people who willingly and freely, by the power of love, desire and do His will.

Praying, "Amaze us, O God," at its deepest level is a

cry from your heart to know this amazing God who does unbelievably amazing things. We become participants with Him in fulfilling His plan and our destiny as He reveals His infinite power, His gracious nature, and His boundless love by His mighty acts.

These almighty acts, a sampling of which has been recounted in this writing, are extensions of His never-ending love toward us. When He amazes us, we need to learn to focus on the giver more than the gift, otherwise we are in danger of becoming sign-seekers rather than searchers reaching for the incomparable God behind the signs. This is one reason that what are often called "supernatural revivals" dissipate and die, leaving those who have witnessed their mighty acts to wonder, "Where has God gone?" They can only be maintained and increased by a progressive, insatiable hunger for Him.

A Resting Place of Potential and Dreams

I at one time had a ranch in the beautiful hills of the Cumberland Plateau in central Tennessee. On this ranch were the remains of eleven pioneer homesteads—mostly stone rubble foundations and a couple dilapidated wood dwellings that in their prime did not even approach the comfort or amenities of the garage where I now shelter my car.

On this ranch were several burial plots and a small cemetery, which housed the final remains of the early stouthearted inhabitants of this backwoods country. As I walked past the cemetery, I would often think of those lying within the dusty forgotten graves and recollect that upon the death of each there must have been a great sense of loss and separation for those who remained behind. No doubt, they laid their loved ones into the ground with many tears and fond memories.

The simple headstones—some of which were battered and broken, with the names on many washed almost beyond recognition by years of weathering—told only the identity of the final possessors of these small four-foot-by-eight-foot sections of earth and the date of their birth and departure. Occasionally there would be some small epitaph or scripture placed as a parting word by someone who cherished the person whose earthly remains were forever placed into that now vanishing field.

These markers provided me a brief glimpse of middle-aged mothers, old men, and various folk who once inhabited the land over which I, at that time, held ownership. I could see grave markers of infant children who never grew to discover or even view the world into which they were born and whole families whose dates of death were so near to each other that they must have died in some fire or plague or unfortunate accident.

Now after these many years, there is no one left to mourn them or even care for their vanishing graves. No picture of what they looked like remained; no record of the kind of people they were or the history of their journey survived. Their desires, their potential, and their dreams had all vanished. Within another couple of generations, any earthly memory of them, like their rapidly crumbling graves, would probably turn to dust.

So it is as the Bible informs us, "He knoweth our frame; he remembereth that we are dust. As for man, his days are as grass: as a flower of the field, so he flourisheth. For the wind passeth over it, and it is gone; and the place thereof shall know it no more" (Psalms 103:14–16). Our eternal value, then, is not in our flesh that perishes but in our spirit that remains.

Were these people of faith able to come out of their graves and stand on the ground they once cultivated and over which they toiled, they would be amazed—amazed by what their little homesteads had become and by the technology of modern invention.

Yet I doubt they would be amazed by our emotional and spiritual progress. I doubt they would embrace the marvelous technology of our day if they also had to give reception to the moral decay that has accompanied much of our social and material evolution. Of course this is a moot point since they no longer exist in the flesh but in the spirit. Perhaps from their vantage point, their message would be of spiritual things and of an amazing God.

Our spirit is what comes from God and that part of us that knows God and is eternal. Our spirit is indestructible and lives forever. In this book I have shared many amazing stories, the purpose of which was not only to say that God desires to be active in our daily lives, but more important to say that His superlative nature is waiting to be discovered by each of us in ever-increasing ways. I think my father, were he still alive, would agree as well.

The Spirit Gives Life

I always felt a strange, sad blending of compassion and resigned reality each time I went to the rest home to be with my dad. Room 56 always came up much too soon, and I noticed an involuntary hesitation each time I approached that yellow varnished door. Time had used her tools well, and I knew that once again my memory of that wonderfully strong and gentle man was about to be repossessed by the truth of that moment.

He was often in his wheelchair. On one visit I saw him stiff at the hips and knees, as he sat somewhat slumped and to the side, but secured in that position by a bedsheet tied around his upper body. He was fumbling with the knot when I came into the room. Without any sign of recognition, he asked me to deliver him from this terrible bondage. Then he looked up at me again and with enormous emotion said, "Well, Luke, where have you been? I've been out looking for you all night!" (Luke was his older brother.)

"Daddy, this is Mark."

He answered, "Oh yes," and as he pulled my hand toward his face, he kissed it over and over and softly began to weep. Struggling through the fog of his advancing dementia, he knows me. I am Mark. I am his son.

Slumped in that chair, battling to stay awake in my world, was the man who pioneered and established more than twenty churches. Here was the brave heart who, at my age, sold our farm, furniture, tools, and toys to move to a spiritually barren part of the Northeast and begin again because he "couldn't find anyone younger who would go."

Often when I was with him, we would sing old hymns and quote Scripture together. Alzheimer's took his mind, but his spirit was free. Though in his advancing condition he lost all recognition of the world around him, his spirit man—the part of us that knows God and communicates with Him—was very much alive and able to speak into the earthly world through Scripture. Ultimately, the flesh profits little but the spirit always gives life. Maybe it is wisdom not to be too tied to the flesh of those we love but to never let go of the spirit or who they are.

I cried over his flesh, as we all do when someone close to us dies. But I also rejoiced and continue to rejoice over his spirit, which is alive, and over the fruit that lives on in the love of God that he was able to impart to his world and to future generations by those who were influenced by the God who was within him.

Though he is now gone—as is my mother, as are a multitude of those who have gone on before us who have carried in their day the seeds of truth—they provide for our generation a foundation to help connect us to our eternal God. We are but one generation in a string of many that will eventually restore the earth and all that is in it to the rule of God.

Flesh only has value while it is alive, but while alive we have the ability to affect our world for good. Money, material possessions, and even reputations cease to exist over time and are forgotten. What we leave the world that lasts is whatever God has given us that we have been able to place within our children and others. It is this that carries on into the future and becomes our eternal testimony. So the person of wisdom learns that this world is governed by the spiritual and that the spiritual person can help restore all life and this material world to the order of God.

Life is a great gift. This world, if looked at through

spiritual eyes, is a wonderful place. We should make use of all the privileges and opportunities life affords. While we are alive, we have the ability to manifest God in this dimension. We have an ability to work toward the manifestation of God's Kingdom in the earth by our spiritual transformation into His image.

Realizing this, perhaps our prayer should be, "God, may we amaze You by our love for one another and by a desire for You that is even above our desire for what You can do for us. May the whole earth be filled with the glory of God, and may the God of heaven take His rightful place in full authority as the God of earth as well."

In this we pray, *Amaze us, O God!*

Printed in the United States
By Bookmasters